Healthy, Wealthy, and Wise

Healthy, Wealthy, and Wise

ഇ ൧

*52 Life-Changing Lessons for the
Twenty-first Century*

INSPIRED BY BEN FRANKLIN

Andrea Rains Waggener

 HAZELDEN®

Hazelden
Center City, Minnesota 55012-0176

1-800-328-0094
1-651-213-4590 (Fax)
www.hazelden.org

13-digit ISBN 978-1-59285-154-6

Library of Congress Cataloging-in-Publication Data
Waggener, Andrea Rains, 1960–
    Healthy, wealthy, and wise : 52 life-changing lessons
  for the twenty-first century : inspired by Ben Franklin /
  Andrea Rains Waggener.
      p. cm.
    Includes bibliographical references.
    ISBN 1-59285-154-1 (paperback)
    1. Change (Psychology) 2. Affirmations. 3. Personality
  change. 4. Success. I. Title: 52 life-changing lessons for the
  twenty-first century. II. Title.

BF637.C4W33 2005
179'.9—dc22

                                              2004042357

09 08 07 06 05   6 5 4 3 2

Cover design by David Spohn
Interior design by Rachel Holscher
Typesetting by Stanton Publication Services, Inc.

FOR TIM,

whose love brings out my best qualities

AND FOR MUGGINS,

who has done lamentably little to make me wealthy
but has more than made up for that by helping
me be healthy and wise

Contents

Acknowledgments

MANY THANKS TO THE PEOPLE I MENTION IN THIS BOOK—
people who fill my life with love and wisdom. Without you I
would not be the person I am and this book would not be
what it is. I am honored and appreciate being able to tell
your stories here—stories that teach and inspire. So thank
you all for opening your lives to me, and through me, to others. Thank you, Tim and Muggins—you make every day joyful; thank you, Mom and Dad; thank you, Herb (my father);
thank you, Jan, Jackie, and Dianna—your friendship delights and enriches me; and thank you, Jake, the wonder
dog, for all the smiles.

Thank you also, Karen Chernyaev and Tracy Lutz, my editors at Hazelden. You made the publishing process fun and
easy.

Introduction

MANY YEARS AGO, I DECIDED I WANTED A STEP BOX TO USE for step aerobics, which was just beginning to catch on in popularity. Unwilling to go out and spend the money to buy a step box, I decided to build one. How hard could it be? It was just a rectangular wooden box. Even though I'd never built anything before, I figured I could handle such a simple project.

I happened to have a sheet of particleboard left over from some household project, and I decided to use it for the box. I had nails, and I had a bone saw. A saw is a saw, right? I thought I could make do with it.

After I determined the dimensions of my box, I carefully measured the particleboard and outlined the pieces I needed to cut. Then I got to work with my small saw.

That's when the trouble started.

A bone saw, I discovered, is not the right tool for cutting particleboard. Determined still, I sawed away with the bone saw until I had cut out my pieces. When I was done, though, the edges were jagged and uneven.

I can still make it work, I thought. Resolutely, I got out my hammer and the nails and began pounding the pieces together. The nails weren't quite long enough and I hadn't cut any supports for the corners so the joints were loose and unstable. But I doggedly kept at it. I finally got the box together. In the end, though, I wasn't pleased with the result. I had a crooked box that wobbled dangerously every time I stepped on it.

Disappointed, I set the box aside. The next time my stepfather (Dad) came to visit, I showed it to him and asked whether he could help me make a better box. He stared in amazement at my pitiful excuse for a box and said, "That's a mess. You didn't have the right tools or materials. I'll make you a box."

And he did.

It's constructed of thick plywood. Dad cut out the box pieces using his band saw, and he put it together with screws drilled into support brackets at the corners. The box is stable and sturdy, and I still use it more than ten years later.

Life is like a step box. To build a good one, you need the right tools and materials. For life, of course, band saws, drills, plywood, and screws won't work. The right tools and materials for a great life are the qualities you develop within yourself to guide your conduct as you go through your days.

Benjamin Franklin knew the value of using the right tools to guide his conduct. When he was a young man, he drew up a list of what he called "virtues." He started with twelve. When a friend pointed out to Franklin that Franklin was rather smug about his own merits, Franklin added a thirteenth virtue: humility. Franklin then set up a thirteen-week course for practicing his virtues. Each week he focused on one virtue, and he marked down in a diary the progress he made toward practicing that virtue. He repeated the thirteen-week course four times a year.[1]

When I first heard of Franklin's virtues, I was inspired. Benjamin Franklin was an amazing man—a forward-thinker, a man of great intellect, creativity, drive, and passion. Franklin was as he preached: healthy, wealthy, and wise. I wanted to develop in myself whatever it took to have a life as full and productive as his was. So I decided I needed to take a look at my own conduct and set up some guidelines.

I thought Franklin's list of virtues, though laudable, were a bit dated. I also thought the list wasn't complete. So I came up with my own list, choosing virtues I believe are necessary to create a rich, full, and happy life.

Instead of calling the items on my list "virtues," I call them "qualities." I like the double meaning of the word *quality,* which is defined as both a characteristic of something or someone *and* a level of excellence. When you have certain characteristics, or qualities, you create that excellence, or quality, in your life. And when you create that excellence and quality, you transform your inner self.

This book is a collection of fifty-two qualities that will help you build a life of excellence. Borrowing Franklin's idea, the qualities are set up as a fifty-two-week course, one quality per week. Each week, you will read a discussion of what it means to have the quality and how you can get it. You will then apply, each day, one of the seven suggestions for creating that quality in your life. At the end of the year, you will have worked on all fifty-two qualities. You may do this program just once, or you can do it every year, as Franklin did. I work this program all the time. Many of these qualities are tough ones to create, and they take continued effort, but struggling through your days takes effort too. Why not use your energy to transform your life instead of wasting your energy doing the same old things to get the same old results?

The first three days of each week, you will do the same tasks for each quality: ask for it, affirm it, and act as if you have the quality. On day 1, you will ask for the quality. You will put a request out to the universe for the quality or, if you're more comfortable praying, you'll say a prayer asking God for the ability to have the quality. Just remember, you won't magically be given the quality. You'll be given situations that allow you to practice developing the quality. Ask the universe or God to help you learn the quality from situations you experience with clarity, not confusion. You'll be amazed at how you'll be given gentle opportunities to develop the quality you're working on.

On day 2, you will affirm your desire for the quality. Say "I am [the quality you're working on]" several times throughout the day. You need to begin thinking of yourself as having that quality. Saying "I am [the quality you're working on]" will help you do this.

On day 3, you will act as if you have the quality. Maybe you don't have the quality you're working on yet. That's okay. On day 3 you will play "let's pretend"—"Let's pretend I'm [the quality you're working on]." Pretend you are a person who has that quality. As you go through the day, be like an actor playing a role. Play the role of a person who has the quality. What would a person with that quality do? Act that way. It may feel unnatural at first, but the more you do it, the more natural it will become. Eventually, you will no longer be role-playing. You will have the quality you're working on.

As you read about and practice the qualities in this book,

you'll notice some of the qualities may seem to contradict others on the list. For instance, the quality of being present would seem to be inconsistent with being goal-oriented. How can you have all the qualities at the same time? Why would you want to?

Well, let's go back to the step box. In order to build that box, Dad needed tools that were, when you think about it, inconsistent with each other. Saws cut things down so you can take them apart. Screws hold things together. Obviously, though, Dad needed the different tools for the different parts of his project.

Qualities work the same way. To build a quality life, a life of excellence like the sturdy box my dad built for me, you will need different tools for different times. Sometimes you will need to be determined, and sometimes you will need to be patient. Sometimes you will want to be strong, and sometimes you will want to be playful.

While some of the qualities will seem at odds with each other, others will seem quite similar. Purposeful and intentional, for example, are almost the same—almost, but not quite. Think of the tools for the step box again. I learned that all saws are not the same. A bone saw and a band saw may be similar, but the effect of each is quite different. The same is true of a flathead screwdriver and a Phillips screwdriver. Some qualities have subtle differences. If you practice them all, you'll have just the right one you need for whatever comes your way in life.

The key to building excellence is having all the tools and learning when to use each one. Developing the fifty-two qualities in this book will put all the tools you need for a quality life at your fingertips. Practicing them weekly will give you the experience you need so you'll know when to use each quality to create the excellent life you want.

I have organized the book alphabetically because the order in which you work on the qualities doesn't matter so much as the work itself. If some qualities call to you more than others, do those first. You can practice the qualities in any order you desire, and having the qualities in alphabetical order will help you easily find the ones you want. The only quality placed out of alphabetical order is joyful, which is placed at the end, because all the other qualities lead up to being joyful. When you develop the qualities in this book and learn to use them well in your life, you'll create a quality life. The bottom line of a quality life is being joyful.

You may notice, by the way, that some obvious qualities are missing from this book—qualities such as happy, exhilarated, exuberant, delighted, triumphant, bubbly, jubilant, vivacious, and energetic. These aren't accidental oversights. These qualities are natural by-products of your inner transformation. They are the *results* of creating your best self.

It may seem like a daunting task at first to develop fifty-two qualities in yourself. As my father-in-law said when I told him about the book, "I have enough trouble with the Ten Commandments. I don't know whether I could keep track of that many qualities." Well, I didn't say it would be easy. But worth the effort? Definitely.

When you develop the qualities in this book, you create a personal advisor/problem solver/cheerleader within yourself who can guide you through every aspect of your life. Before I began working on the qualities in this book, I devoured self-help books and tapes looking for ways to deal with the problems I faced and searching for advice on how to get what I wanted from life. I thought someone out there could tell me what I needed to do. Once I began changing my inner self, however, I found that *I knew* what I needed to do.

I also was better able to do it. Every aspect of my life has improved since I began working on my inner qualities: my health (I've lost a lot of weight and no longer suffer from the extreme mood swings of bipolar disorder), my relationships (I found the love of my life and created a more direct relationship with my parents), my career (I began selling books after years of rejections), and my spiritual life (I feel more at peace and have more joy in my days).

And even though it requires some work, it's not tedious work. This can be a fun process if you take it a day at a time and approach it with an enthusiastic spirit (to learn how to be enthusiastic, check out "Passionate" and "Spirited"). So go ahead and jump in. Spend the next year collecting the tools you need to live the life you've always wanted to lead. Think of it as a scavenger hunt for the best parts of yourself.

Be prepared for some challenges as you embark on transforming your inner self, but don't let those challenges discourage you. Your inner transformation is the key that will unlock the door to excellence in your life experiences. Isn't that worth a little bit of effort?

So transform your inner self. Practice the qualities. Grab that key.

A quality life is waiting for you.

Accepting

Accepting looks at what it sees without judgment. It doesn't put labels on things. Accepting has friends of every color and religion. It walks on both sides of the tracks. Accepting doesn't decide whether something is bad or good. Accepting allows what is to be what is.

MANY YEARS AGO, WHEN I WAS WAY TOO YOUNG FOR MY own good, was skinny, and thought I knew it all, I would look at obese people and wonder how they could possibly have let themselves go so badly. *Fat people had to be weak people,* I figured. If they were strong and had the will to control themselves, they wouldn't be fat. When it came to fat people, I was judge and jury, and they were convicted of not being okay.

I didn't stop at judging fat people. I had similar judgments for people who were messy, people who were slow in either thought or action, people who were uncouth. I was so full of judgments that I couldn't look at a person without finding something wrong with him or her.

This included me. I couldn't look at myself without finding something wrong. Even though I was skinny, my waist wasn't narrow enough. Even though I was smart, my memory wasn't good enough.

My eyes didn't know how to look at the world and just see it as it is. My eyes knew only how to judge.

To my credit, I never judged people on the basis of their skin color or religion. I wasn't prejudiced. I was simply judgmental across the board.

Then I grew up. I also gained a lot of weight.

Although I can't say I'm thrilled that I gained weight when I hit my mid-thirties, I can say I'm happy with the lesson it taught me. It showed me how much I judge myself and others. From that point on, I focused on giving up judgments, and I began to learn to be accepting.

Being accepting means looking at every human being you encounter and celebrating that person, not judging him or her. When you're accepting, you don't look for what's wrong or what's right; you look for what is. As I talk about in "Adaptable," when you're accepting, you can experience events and situations without judging them as good or bad. You can have an attitude of "Hmm, I wonder what will come from this" instead of "Oh no, this is terrible."

When you're accepting, you don't decide people are better or worse than you are; you remember that they are the same as you. In fact, you know they're connected to you. Our world is made up of energy. You, me, and every animate and inanimate object in the world is made up of energy. This energy, scientists now know, is all connected. You may seem to be separate from others, but you're not. Therefore, how can you possibly do anything but accept everyone you meet? In accepting others, you accept yourself.

To fully accept others and yourself, you need to give up comparisons. Don't look to see whether your lawn is greener than your neighbors' and judge either yourself or your neighbor accordingly. Just look at the different lawns and accept that they are what they are. They're just lawns of varying color.

Judgment breeds separation and hate. If you think you're better than someone else, it's easy to treat him or her with disrespect and even cruelty. If you think someone is better than you, you'll allow yourself to be treated with disrespect and cruelty.

Acceptance celebrates connectedness and creates love. When you see people just as people, not as either good or bad, you will treat people with care and love.

If you want to live in a loving world, if you want to see the beauty in everyone you meet and everything you encounter, learn to accept. Accept others and accept yourself.

ʊ Becoming Accepting

Day 1: Ask to be accepting.

Day 2: Affirm your desire to become accepting.

Day 3: Act as if you're accepting.

Day 4: Notice how often you judge people. Do you criticize clothing choices or hair color or mannerisms? If so, make an effort to turn those criticisms into benign observations. "What a stupid hairstyle" becomes "That's an interesting hairstyle."

Day 5: Notice how often you compare yourself to others. Do you look at what others are doing at your workplace, for instance, and feel bad if they're doing better or feel smug if they're doing worse? If so, make an effort to give up comparisons.

Day 6: Visualize a stream of energy connecting you with the people you see. You can also imagine a stream of energy connecting you with people you're interacting with, even if you don't see them. Imagine that energy flowing between you and the person you're talking to over the phone or communicating with via e-mail. It will remind you that we are all connected and that all of us are equally worthy.

Day 7: Make a list of any prejudices you have. Even if you're accepting of other races and religions, are you perhaps prejudiced against bad drivers or people who take drugs? Listing your prejudices will make you more aware of your judgments. When you're done with your list, destroy it. Let go of your ideas of what's right and wrong with people.

Adaptable

Adaptable is always ready to change directions at the drop of a hat. It is never lost because it's okay with wherever it is. Adaptable is a renaissance trait, a jack-of-all-trades. It's happy to be fast or slow or free or restricted. Adaptable doesn't fight or resist change. It doesn't get stuck on what it can't have but joyfully embraces what it does have.

A COUPLE YEARS AGO, MY SPRINGER SPANIEL, MUGGINS, was diagnosed with inflammatory bowel disease. After a couple scary flare-ups that required hospitalization, our veterinarian told us it was imperative Muggins not eat crab shells. Unfortunately, Muggins often ate crab shells before I could stop her when we took our daily walks on the beach. So I had three choices: not take her to the beach at all, leash her while there, or muzzle her. I chose a muzzle.

When I first put the muzzle on Muggins, she was quite put out. She glared at me in disbelief. Then she started jumping around like a bronco bucking out of the starting gate at a rodeo. She writhed and leaped and pawed at her face.

This lasted a couple minutes while I looked on, cringing and feeling like the meanest dog mom in the world. Then

Muggins suddenly stopped fighting. She shook herself one last time and snorted. I could see her reach a conclusion: *Well, I guess I have to wear this dumb thing, but at least I'm on the beach. So I guess I'll just ignore the thing and go have some fun.* And off she trotted down the beach, tail wagging, ears perked, nose in the air. *That,* I thought, *was one of the best displays of adaptability I've ever seen.*

Adaptability is the capacity to accept the changes and challenges you face. It is an ability to go with the flow.

Most people have trouble going with the flow. They expend way too much energy resisting changes or new limitations. For example, I used to be quite slender. I wore a size ten or sometimes a twelve. Walking, standing, and moving in general was easy. Then, for a variety of reasons, I gained a lot of weight, and walking, standing, and moving in general became more difficult.

At first, like Muggins did with her muzzle, I resisted this change to my body. I was so focused on how awful it felt to be fat that I missed every single thing in my life that was good. I was caught up in what was wrong, and I couldn't see what was right.

But finally and thankfully—although not as quickly—I adapted, like Muggins. I accepted that my body wasn't what it used to be. I began looking for what was right about my body, like the fact that my breasts were now full and voluptuous and the fact that having more meat on my bones kept me warm at night.

Life is full of shocking change. If you resist it, you won't handle it well. You'll grumble and complain. In essence, you'll metaphorically buck around and fight the changes. When you do this, you deprive yourself of joy and waste a lot of energy. If Muggins had kept fighting her muzzle, she wouldn't have been able to go on her beach walk, which is one of her greatest joys.

When you're busy fighting and resisting, you miss the pleasure in life. If you want to enjoy every moment, you must be adaptable. You can use what you learn in "Accepting" to help you be adaptable. Instead of judging what occurs in your life, accept it. It isn't good or bad. It just is. Take away your judgment, and it's easier to accept change and live with situations you'd rather not live with. The interesting thing is that when you relax and accept something you don't like, it tends to go away faster. Muggins no longer wears a muzzle. She learned that if she doesn't eat crab shells, she doesn't have to be muzzled. Yet again, she's adapted.

When you feel like you've been muzzled by some change you don't like, take a lesson from Muggins. You need to shake it off and move on. The fun in life is still there. You just have to focus on it. Accept what is. Adapt.

ᔕ Becoming Adaptable

Day 1: Ask to be adaptable.

Day 2: Affirm your desire to become adaptable.

Day 3: Act as if you're adaptable.

Day 4: Make a list of things in your life you resist. Notice how much time you spend thinking about things on this list and feeling angry, resentful, or frustrated about them.

Day 5: Make a list of the things you enjoy doing. How many can you still do, even though you've been limited by some muzzle (such as lack of money, long work hours, or an injury)? Today make a decision to focus on what you have, not on what you've lost.

Day 6: Write out what you feel about situations or limitations you're resisting. For example, about my getting fat, I would write, "I hate being fat. It makes me feel so awful and ashamed. I'm miserable. Why did this happen? It's not fair." Pour your resistance out onto the page. When you're done, tear up the paper. Tell yourself you're ready to let go of your resistance to this situation or limitation. Now you can adapt to the change.

Day 7: Physically shake off your resistance. Think of something you're resisting. Then thrash around a little, kind of like a dog trying to shake off a muzzle. (Do this in bed or someplace where you won't hurt yourself.) Now take a deep breath, stretch, and smile. Stand up straight. This is the physical stance of being adaptable.

Adventurous

Adventurous rides a spirited horse and gallops into new things with enthusiastic abandon. Adventurous will parachute out of a plane, visit a foreign country, try new cuisine, and wear funky clothes in colors that have obscure names like chartreuse. Adventurous loves to start new projects, and it sees these projects through the eyes of a child with a fistful of crayons and a stack of construction paper. Adventurous seeks out challenges. Adventurous dances every dance.

I USED TO THINK I WASN'T ADVENTUROUS. I THINK IT would be fun to learn to parachute and I like fast things such as roller coasters and sports cars, but for the most part, my life is pretty tame. I don't go on adventures, unless you call walking the dog alongside the ocean an adventure.

You probably don't call that an adventure. And you'd be right, unless, for you, walking alone is difficult to do. If it's something you've never done before, or if you're afraid of it and you do it anyway, then it is most assuredly an adventure.

My husband, Tim, and I got together in an unorthodox way. We had dated for a while just after high school, but we lost touch with each other. I married someone else. So did he. We lived separate lives, each of us thinking of the other from time to time but never contacting each other.

Then, twenty years after we last saw each other, I had a whim to find Tim. The notion came out of nowhere, but I followed it (see the whole story in "Intuitive"). When I found him, he was on the other side of the country. We communicated for a month. Then he left his failed marriage and moved across the country to be with me. We decided to live together based on a month of phone and electronic communication.

"I sure do admire your sense of adventure," a friend of mine said when I told her what was happening.

Adventure? I didn't think of what I was doing with Tim as an adventure.

"I love," my friend continued, "the way you plunge into new experiences, the way you're willing to try something risky. You are so adventurous."

Really? Me, adventurous? I had never thought of myself that way.

But it's true. Adventure, you see, is about breaking through barriers. These can be societal barriers or self-imposed barriers. Societal barriers have to do with being proper and reasonable or doing the "right" thing. Self-imposed barriers are barriers of fear, shame, or even habit. When you're adventurous, you cast aside your concerns about meeting society's expectations and break through your insecurities. You take risks and have new experiences.

Before Tim moved in with me, an acquaintance of mine warned, "Be careful. For all you know, he could be a serial killer now." I didn't think he was, but it was still a risk for us to move in together without having spent time together first. Would we get along? Would we drive each other crazy?

Tim and I married a little over a year after he moved in. Our relationship has been a roaring success. It's a relationship I never would have had if I hadn't been willing to be adventurous by casting aside the societal barriers of what is proper and breaking through my own fears about failed relationships.

When you define adventurous as breaking through barriers, you will discover you probably have a lot of adventures in your life: new jobs, new skills, new people, and new places to live. Being adventurous only asks that you do something a bit different once in a while. If you want something, be willing to put yourself out there to get it. You may have to live a little dangerously. Risk some money. Risk your heart. If the dream is worth fulfilling, the actions needed to achieve it are worth taking.

ᴥ Becoming Adventurous

Day 1: Ask to be adventurous.

Day 2: Affirm your desire to become adventurous.

Day 3: Act as if you're adventurous.

Day 4: Claim your adventurous side. Think about things you have done in your life or things you're doing now that are adventurous. Where are you taking risks? These are adventures. Give yourself credit for the adventure you're already having.

Day 5: What adventures do you want to have? Make a list of things you'd like to do that require some risk, whether the risk is physical, monetary, or emotional. Do you want to move to a new town? Do you want to learn to sail even though you don't know how to swim? Write down your ideas. If you're going to be adventurous, you need to know what kind of adventures you want to experience.

Day 6: Pick an adventure from your list. Do at least one thing today that will move you toward it. If what you've chosen is a move, for example, look up real estate listings for the new city or check job listings. Even making a list of what you need to do to bring about your adventure is a step.

Day 7: Have a little adventure today. Go to a new restaurant or buy a food you've never tried. Introduce yourself to a stranger. Speak up in a situation where you'd usually remain silent. Take a risk—just a little risk. Bask in how exhilarating it feels to try something new.

Attentive

Attentive is an all-seeing eye. It's an all-hearing ear. It is totally aware and always focused on what's going on around it. Attentive is an alert sentry at the gate. It is a pinpoint of light that lands with laser precision on everything it encounters. Attentive is tough to surprise because it never blinks. Attentive reacts at lightning speed because it is always ready.

MY DOG, MUGGINS, HAS A "BOYFRIEND." HIS NAME IS JAKE, and he belongs to Dianna, a good friend of mine.

I can understand why Muggins loves Jake. He's sweet and loving, cuddly and handsome, gentle and cooperative. But Jake, unfortunately, isn't as enamored of Muggins as she is of him. He doesn't dislike her—it's just that he has other things on his mind. Jake is all about *the ball*. Jake's a yellow lab, and labs live for balls, not for black-and-white springer spaniels who have the hots for them.

Muggins's unrequited love aside, you ought to see Jake rivet his attention on a ball. When you have a ball in your hand, Jake is right there keeping an eye on it. Every nerve ending, every muscle, every cell in Jake's body is focused on your hand. He is rigid and quivering. His ears are perked.

His head is up and cocked to one side. His eyes are bright. His tail is alert. Just try and get that ball past him without him knowing about it. Can't be done.

Okay, so maybe being so focused on balls isn't something to which you need to aspire, but the manner in which Jake focuses on balls is a quality you do need. Jake is a poster-dog for being attentive.

You probably heard it first at home, and then you heard it in school: "Pay attention!"

It was never something you wanted to hear when you were a kid because paying attention often wasn't much fun. It was far more amusing to spin in circles or bounce on the bed than it was to listen to your mother tell you how to fold socks. The spontaneous mind does not like to pay attention.

And there's nothing wrong with the spontaneous mind. It's the doorway to adventure and innovation. But how can the spontaneous mind act on what it comes up with if it doesn't learn and retain what it encounters along the way?

When you get that grand idea for a novel about an underground tunnel that leads to a magical city, it would be helpful if you had paid attention when you were being taught punctuation and sentence structure. When you get the great notion to plant an organic garden in your back-yard, it would be useful if you could remember what your dad taught you about composting.

Attention is like that first handful of snow you grab when you want to build a snowman. If you can't get the first ball of snow going, if it doesn't clump in your hand and start picking up more snow as you roll it, you will never have a snowman.

Attention, as Jake has demonstrated, requires focus. When you're listening, for instance, you need to focus on what you hear. You cannot be thinking about what you need to do later or what you're going to say in response. You need to concentrate. When you listen with attention, you will always be prepared to react and respond to what you hear. Nothing will get past you.

One of the skills they teach police officers and intelligence agents is attention. These people need to see the details of everything around them because the details, like the hand twitch that indicates a knife in someone's back pocket, could save their lives.

In your life, attention won't always be such a life-and-death matter. But it can be. If you're practicing attention, you'll notice the blanket that fell too close to the space heater before the fire starts. You'll see your toddler reaching for the scissors before he or she can grab it.

Whether it's something as simple as knowing what a best friend's favorite meal is or something as complex as knowing how to build an airplane, it all starts with attention. Want success, great relationships, and well-being? Focus, concentrate, and notice the details in life.

Take it from Jake. Life will be a ball if you're attentive.

❧ Becoming Attentive

Day 1: Ask to be attentive.

Day 2: Affirm your desire to become attentive.

Day 3: Act as if you're attentive.

Day 4: Practice listening. When someone is speaking to you, make an effort to focus on the words. Pretend you will be tested on the content. See whether you can get every little detail of what people tell you today.

Day 5: Practice seeing. Whenever you have a moment, stop and look around. Really look. Try and notice all the details of your surroundings. See that little scratch on the base of the table leg? How about that cobweb near the light fixture? Notice color, texture, and shape. Find something that you never noticed before in every familiar place you are in today.

Day 6: Watch people. As often as you can, when you look at a stranger, memorize his or her face. Notice what the person is wearing. Pretend your life depends on imprinting the person's appearance in your mind.

Day 7: Whatever you do today, fully focus on it. Be a stickler for details. Learn all you can from the book you're reading. Really hear the music you listen to. Soak in knowledge and experiences today.

Calm

Calm is easy breathing, a soft belly, and relaxed muscles. It is a mind focused on the wispy colors of sunset and not on the frenzied activity of the boats on the water in front of the sun. Calm is a sense of rightness, of faith, a feeling that all is as it should be or will be again. Calm can create silence amid the greatest clatter. It is a soft whispered "Ahh" that can be heard through the cacophony of life's struggle.

MY DOG, MUGGINS, LOVES TO GO TO THE BEACH — EVERY day. In fact, she insists on going to the beach every day — in sun or in wind and rain. Muggins wants to walk, no matter what. So we walk.

During the winter, most days are either windy or rainy, frequently both, so I have to push through gusts of thirty miles per hour or stronger. I come home soaked and covered with sand. I do this day after day after day. It's my normal morning. The roar of the surf, the rush of the wind — these sounds that fill my head are natural. I'm used to the noise and the struggle.

Once in a while, however, just when I think I can't possibly face another windy day, Mother Nature blesses me with a day of calm. When I look out my window on these rare and wonderful days, I see tree branches hanging perfectly still in bright sunshine. On those days, I sigh with relief and contentment. Instead of struggling through the wind and rain, I take an easy walk along a sparkling blue ocean and breathe in the peace of utter calm. On those days, I fill up my spiritual tank.

Thankfully, inner calm is not in the hands of Mother Nature. The ability to be calm is within you. It's there for you to claim and experience any time you want.

Everybody has experienced calm at some point in their lives, and most people would love to be calm all the time. But many people think that in order to be calm they have to have everything around them just right.

During the last couple of years, I've gone through some rather stressful times. I faced major financial struggles. I was involved in a legal quagmire. My beloved dog was severely ill. My father died. For a while, I kept telling myself to just hang on. I would have calm when the trying times were over. But when they just went on and on, I realized I had to find a way to be calm in the midst of the turmoil. So I began practicing deep breathing. I learned to stop, take a deep and full breath, and go into the silence within instead of reacting with anger or panic to the situation I was in.

I admit this doesn't always work. Sometimes it works for an instant before I go back to hyperventilating and emoting all over the place. Then I catch myself and take another breath. I take myself out of wind and rain that is my life and pull myself into that calm, blue-sky day that is the essence of me. In that place, I remain still and nonreactive to all that goes on around me.

Being calm is a choice. Sure, you can choose to be annoyed by what people do or say. You can choose to be stopped by every little hurdle you encounter. Or you can choose to be calm. When you choose to be calm in your life, all your troubles and challenges don't disappear. In the midst of it all, though, you can find a pocket of stillness.

So take a minute now and then to breathe in calm. If you want to learn to move through your activities and challenges without having them knock you around and flatten you, you must learn to be calm while life's relentless storm rages on around you.

ᴄ BECOMING CALM

Day 1: Ask to be calm.

Day 2: Affirm your desire to become calm.

Day 3: Act as if you're calm.

Day 4: Begin your day with a visualization. Imagine walking on a beach in a raging rainstorm. Feel the sting of the water on your face. Hear the wind's and the surf's roar. Feel your lungs struggling to work as you push into the wind. Now imagine the storm suddenly receding. Breathe in the still, quiet air. Let the surf's murmur soothe you. Enjoy your easy, even breath. Tell yourself you can have this kind of calm any time today. Carry it with you, and when you feel stressed, close your eyes and conjure up the image of this peaceful beach. Let it soothe you.

Day 5: Do something to remind yourself to create calm today. Set your watch to chime each hour or wear a colorful string tied around your wrist—whatever it takes to get your attention. Whenever you hear or see your reminder, take in a deep breath, then blow it out. Do it again. Create a moment of calm in the chaos of your day.

Day 6: When you feel agitated, upset, frustrated, or angry today, remind yourself you have a choice. Say this phrase from *A Course in Miracles:* "I can choose peace rather than this."[2]

Day 7: Practice meditating in a noisy setting. Let the TV blast or the radio blare. Attempt to focus on your breathing. If you learn how to do this, you can create inner calm no matter how raucous your surroundings are.

Centered

Centered is a bull's-eye in the middle of the soul. It is balanced and settled. It is where everything feels okay, even if it isn't. Centered is grounded. It is never rattled or off-kilter. It doesn't wobble. Centered has a magnet that keeps it anchored to truth even when it is surrounded by a swirl of lies. Centered is the core of self.

ONE OF THE HOUSES I USED TO OWN HAD LOVELY HALF-moon windows on either side of a brick fireplace front. When the contractor first installed them, one of the windows was noticeably farther away from the fireplace than the other. Given that the fireplace was centered between two walls, having one of the windows off-center looked pretty bad. I made the contractor take the windows out and redo them. Having things centered is important to me.

Being centered myself is even more important.

I know it immediately when I'm not centered: I'm easily rattled, annoyed, and otherwise bothered. I have no flow in my days. I feel no sense of grace or peace. I am, like the windows in my old house, just a bit off.

So what is being centered?

Well, your soul is at your core. It's the center of your

being, the focal point. Think of yourself as a human dart-board. The numbered sections are parts of your personality and parts of your life. The bull's-eye is your soul. It's your center. When you're in sync with your soul, at peace with yourself and your truth, you're centered.

About fifteen years ago, I first learned what it meant to be centered, and I realized I hadn't been centered for a long time. First, I wasn't okay with myself at all. I looked confident enough, but inside I was a mass of self-doubt. It took me years to look within, accept, and own all aspects of myself, even those that society might disapprove of.

Second, I couldn't focus on my truth because I didn't know what my truth was. Again, it took a long time before I realized that your truth is what makes sense to you—what is comfortable and feels right to you. It's an instinct. When you're in the right place for you, the place that fits like Cinderella's shoe on her tiny foot, you're in your truth. When you're living in ways that look right but don't feel right or in ways that please others but not yourself, you are not in your truth.

When I was in my twenties, I was most assuredly not in my truth. I was in a marriage, in a town, and in a job that felt like strains to me. I was pleasing my parents, my husband, and society. But *I* wasn't pleased at all. Now that I live a life that suits me, I'm living my truth.

Third, when I first learned about being centered, I was in no way aligned with my soul's purpose. I didn't even know what my purpose was. I was in a legal career I hated because I'd always done what I'd been programmed to do. I now know I'm meant to be a writer, meant to share my life experiences with others.

Now I am centered, for the most part. Sure, I get knocked off-center a bit from time to time. I doubt myself or I question my truth or my purpose. Something happens to make me unsure. When it does, though, I am able to recognize it because it feels so awful. I quickly take steps to move back toward my center. I journal. I meditate. I read spiritual books. I take my cosmic dart off the edge of the board and fire it right back at the center. Then life starts flowing again.

If you want flow in your life, if you want to easily move through challenges and brush off stress, you need to be centered. Learn to be okay with yourself. Know your truth. Find your purpose. Keep your life centered and everything else will balance out just right.

∽ BECOMING CENTERED

Day 1: Ask to be centered.

Day 2: Affirm your desire to become centered.

Day 3: Act as if you're centered.

Day 4: Do you like yourself? If so, great. Celebrate yourself today. Give yourself a lot of compliments. Buy yourself a treat. If you don't like yourself, celebrate yourself anyway. But also take some time to make a list of things about yourself of which you're proud. Then celebrate again. Tell yourself you're okay.

Day 5: Begin to figure out your truth. What do you like? Think about all aspects of your life. Do you like where you live, what you wear and eat, what car you drive, what people you spend time with, your job, your leisure activities? Do you do what you do for yourself or for others? Ask yourself what pleases you.

Day 6: Do you know your soul's purpose? If you don't, commit to finding out what it is. What tugs at you? A particular hobby or career? Being a good parent? Your longings will give you clues to your purpose. Write them down.

Day 7: Get one of those inexpensive dartboards with the blunt-tipped darts. Put it up someplace in your house. Position a dart right in the center, in the bull's-eye. If you don't want to be so literally visual, draw a bull's-eye and paste up the drawing. These images will remind you to check each day to see whether you're centered on your truth and your purpose.

Childlike

Childlike is a giggle, the delight in a rainy day and a muddy puddle. Childlike has wide, eager eyes ready to drink in experiences and try new things. It is sweet energy, soft and gentle. Childlike acts from love and embraces everything as a possible adventure. It hugs everything. Childlike never has to try. It just does and then delights in the doing.

THE DAY MY FATHER DIED, MY HUSBAND AND I DROVE TO California to handle my father's affairs. In addition to being in shock over my father's sudden death, I was exhausted during that trip. I was stuck smack in the middle of the obligation and pain of being an adult, and I was almost physically ill from the intensity of it.

But in a small convenience store somewhere in Oregon, where we stopped to get gas in the early hours of the morning, I found something that pulled me back into the child within me that needed comfort and wanted a little fun, even in the middle of my pain. I found what the display called a "stress ball," a ball just a little smaller than a tennis ball that was spongy enough to squeeze easily. I didn't care about that though. What drew me to the ball was its bright yellow color and the impish little smiley face painted on the side.

The ball cost $1.50, and it provided me with hours of fun during what was otherwise a traumatic, stressful, and horrifying trip. I squeezed it. I tossed it around. I delighted in that silly yellow ball, and while I did, I was a kid, allowing myself to be vulnerable and hurt. Sure, I still had to be an adult. I had to arrange for my father's cremation, handle his affairs, and cope with the awful aftermath of the extreme circumstances of his death. But while I was being an adult, I was also being childlike, and the kid in me got me through the ordeal with my sanity intact.

Advertisers and psychologists agree—inside you is a kid. That kid is your connection with being childlike.

Many people rely on their real children to help them find their child within. Joining with children to build cities out of blocks or have tea parties with teddy bears allows you to reconnect to the kid inside you. But you don't need to have kids to be a kid yourself.

Note that there's a difference between being childlike and being childish. Being childish is being immature, selfish to the point of disregarding others, irresponsible, and unwilling to work when necessary or take on obligations. You don't have to be any of these things to be childlike. You can be mature and responsible and still be childlike.

Being childlike is having a real connection with your inner child. Children have spirit and enthusiasm. They know how to experience real joy. They are, at least as long as they're raised in a safe and loving environment, eager and excited about trying new things. They're easily delighted. They love fun. They're full of smiles.

Children don't have an agenda. They may set out to play tag and get sidetracked by a fuzzy caterpillar. They may sit down to read a book and then decide to build a tent from the book for their action figures instead. This ability to be present in the moment is what allows children to live in joy and be passionate about the world. It comes naturally to most kids. Most adults, however, have to work at it a bit. You need to find a kid-vehicle, something you love that brings out the child in you.

I, for example, collect stuffed animals. Bears and other plush animals live all over my house. Winnie-the-Pooh reminds me to trust and be ready for adventure. A big, bright yellow chick named Happy sits in one of the dining room chairs and reminds me to smile when I'm feeling down.

Childish?

No. Childlike.

Being childlike brings giggles into your life. It will comfort you and sustain you through the all-too-adult parts of your time in this world.

When you were a child, you probably couldn't wait to become an adult. But once you became an adult, you found out life was hard for adults. Getting back in touch with the kid you left behind is what will get you through the hard stuff. Being childlike is your anchor to joy in a sea of struggle. Whatever you do, don't let go of that kid in you. He or she will keep you afloat.

∽ Becoming Childlike

Day 1: Ask to be childlike.

Day 2: Affirm your desire to become childlike.

Day 3: Act as if you're childlike.

Day 4: Introduce yourself to your inner child. Ask him or her to tell you what he or she wants. Does he or she want more playtime? More sleep? The occasional chocolate chip cookie? Find out, and then do your best to give your inner child something he or she wants.

Day 5: Buy something silly today: a toy or maybe a stuffed animal. Buy it without feeling self-conscious or guilty. Let your inner child delight in the purchase.

Day 6: Turn something you need to do today into something a little silly. For example, while you're sorting papers at your desk, make a paper-clip sculpture. When you're on the treadmill, pretend you're marching through the jungle on a grand adventure.

Day 7: Read a children's book or watch a children's movie. Find joy in a simple, happy story.

Committed

Committed rides a steady horse, strong and reliable. Committed stays on track, even when the course is muddy and the skies are filled with thunderheads. Committed loves fully and for always. Committed is trustworthy. It can be counted on. It's always there, like a favorite easy chair squatting in the corner of the living room at the end of a long day. Committed sticks around.

WHEN I WAS THIRTY YEARS OLD, I MADE A DECISION TO become a writer. That goal became one of my most important commitments. Writing became my path. But along this path, I found many temptations. There was, for instance, the promise of riches offered from a multi-level marketing company that sold a product I really liked. For more than a year, I set aside my writing to become an entrepreneur. Not surprisingly, I failed because the marketing company wasn't my path, and in following it, I had strayed from the path to which I was committed.

Commitment is like a high-tech missile. Once it locks on target, it stays on track no matter how many twists and turns it may make.

Being committed is a must in all areas of your life. Of

course, you need to be committed to your relationships if you want them to last, but before you even tackle a long-term relationship, you need to be committed to yourself.

Being committed to yourself requires that you stand by yourself through whatever you face. You must be committed to being who you are and doing what you are drawn to do. When you're going after a goal, for example, you must stick to your plan to get there. You must believe that getting there is possible, and you cannot allow doubt to pull you off course. Being committed to yourself means you're determined to build the life you want. You'll do what's necessary to be healthy, to be successful, and to have the comforts and the triumphs you desire.

You probably have had or will have a time in your life when you forget your commitment to yourself. I certainly have gone through such times.

After I was divorced from my first husband, for example, I got involved with a man who was immature, volatile, and full of anger. I got involved with him because I was lonely and I looked to him to fill me up. He desired me and that was all I needed to invite him into my life. Once he got in my life, however, I realized he was all wrong for me. I was so concerned, though, about not hurting his feelings or making him angry that I broke my commitment to myself. I became horribly unhappy because I let him pull me away from my best life.

The irony of commitment is that sometimes you have to break one commitment to keep another. This means you have to prioritize commitments. Being true to yourself must be number one. Then you have to decide for yourself what matters most to you. Is it work? Your creative or spiritual life? Your spouse? Your children? Once you decide, you must take action accordingly.

If you have to break a commitment, and sometimes you will, do so as honorably and responsibly as possible. Tell the truth to whomever you're letting down, and do what it takes to clean up any mess you might leave behind.

Commitment requires that you not allow outside forces to pull you off your path. Once you determine what your path is, you stay on it, even if you happen to see a beautiful rainbow off to the left or a pile of gold off to the right. You know your destination is straight ahead, and it is your choice— the choice you made for yourself and the choice that you have committed yourself to, no matter what.

A commitment is a promise you make, often to others, but always to yourself. If you can't keep promises to yourself, you won't be able to keep those you make to others. If you can't hold a job or stick to an exercise plan, how do you expect to stay in a marriage? Before you make a promise, ask yourself whether you can stay committed to it. Once you commit to anything, you must line up your actions with that promise and avoid all actions inconsistent with it.

When you were born, you were born committed to life. As long as you honor that commitment, you have time to learn to be committed to everything else that matters to you, including committing to living a quality life.

ꙩ Becoming Committed

Day 1: Ask to be committed.

Day 2: Affirm your desire to become committed.

Day 3: Act as if you're committed.

Day 4: Before you make a promise today, from something as small as saying you'll take out the trash to something as big as committing to a new job, ask yourself whether you can keep your promise. Can you stay committed to what you say you'll do? In other words, will you keep your word? If you don't think so, don't make the promise.

Day 5: Make a list of your commitments, both to yourself and others. List your commitments to health, to people, to work. Then prioritize them. Knowing what matters most to you will help you keep your commitments.

Day 6: Pay attention to your actions today. Are they consistent with the promises you've made? Did you, for instance, say you'd go to your daughter's ball game and then go to a meeting instead? If you're acting inconsistently with your promises, you need to make different choices.

Day 7: Notice the temptations that come your way as you try to stay on track with your commitments. Money and romance, for example, are biggies. Write down the things that tempt you. Ask yourself whether they're really worth breaking promises you've made. Often they're not. Sometimes, however, they are, and if they are, end your old commitment honorably and consciously make a new one.

Compassionate

Compassionate sees pain, understands it, and then embraces it. Compassionate is a gentle whisper of truth. It is a warm embrace, a soft murmur of encouragement, a sympathetic smile. Compassionate can be a subtle push or a sweet suggestion. Compassionate is the ability to see another's struggle and allow it to be, without pity.

I'VE ALWAYS THOUGHT I WAS COMPASSIONATE. FOR A LONG time, however, I practiced a distorted version of compassion. My idea of compassion was actually pity that created a need to jump in and "make things right." When I was trying to be compassionate, I would sit and commiserate with people: oh yes, life is lousy, woe is you. Or I'd try and fix them. They needed help. They were doing it all wrong, and I could make it all better.

Well, when I acted this way, I wasn't being compassionate. My actions were judgment and control dressed up in a pretty disguise. When I began to realize that, I also noticed that when I did things because I felt sorry for someone, I tended to get myself in bad situations.

When I was in high school, this girl followed me everywhere. She was painfully shy and had no other friends. I didn't want to be mean, so I never told her I didn't want to hang out with her, even though I didn't particularly like her. But she became a constant shadow, and eventually it got on my nerves. So one day I told her I wasn't happy having her around. I tried to do it nicely but of course she was hurt and I felt like a jerk. We began avoiding each other.

Time passed, and I saw she'd joined the theater group in our school. I'd encounter her in the halls and was pleased that she looked so much more alive than she had when she'd hung out with me. She seemed happy. It appeared she'd found her niche and had a group of friends. In our senior year, we finally reconnected, and she astounded me by telling me I'd done her a huge favor. When I'd told her the truth, she was forced to find her own way—and she did. She discovered she was more than she thought she was.

At the time, I thought I was being compassionate by allowing her to hang around. What I was really doing, though, was feeling sorry for her. The real compassion came when I kindly told her the truth. Then she was free to do what she needed to do.

That's what compassion is: understanding and gentle truth. You're not pitying people, trying to fix them, or giving them what they want because they've had a hard time. You're simply being encouraging in a truthful way. Compassion is helping people discover they're stronger than they think they are and helping them to find the lessons in their experiences.

This kind of compassion is important to give to yourself as well. Being compassionate isn't a weakness. It's not sitting around feeling sorry for yourself. It is gentleness, quiet understanding, and truth. When you're compassionate to yourself, you acknowledge your struggles, remind yourself of your strengths, and gently nudge yourself toward a better place. When you practice treating yourself and others this way, you will naturally be compassionate.

↪ BECOMING COMPASSIONATE

Day 1: Ask to be compassionate.

Day 2: Affirm your desire to become compassionate.

Day 3: Act as if you're compassionate.

Day 4: Notice whether you pity anyone today. Are you judging someone or trying to fix them under the guise of compassion? If so, catch yourself . . . and stop.

Day 5: When you encounter someone in pain or facing a challenge today, don't treat them as if they're weak. Help them see that they are strong enough to face the struggle. Tell them gently that you empathize with their pain but you believe in their ability to get through it.

Day 6: If you really want to be compassionate, listen with your heart. Then tell the truth. People who are hurting don't need to hear lies. They need to hear encouragement. Practice being a cheerleader instead of a commiserator.

Day 7: Be sure you're being compassionate with yourself. If you're struggling with big challenges, pat yourself on the back for your effort. Remind yourself of your strengths. List them. Now list ways you can use those strengths to meet the challenges you face. Do all of this gently. Don't push yourself. Just nudge.

Own

Your

Struggles

Confident

Confident is a massive oak that has stood for decades against all onslaughts. Confidence stands tall, committed to its place in the world. It is sure in its knowledge that it has something to offer. It knows its strengths, acknowledges its weaknesses, and accepts its whole self with aplomb. Confident sings its own song at the top of its lungs and expects the song will be enjoyed by at least one person who understands.

A FEW YEARS AGO DURING A COUCH POTATO MOMENT OF mindless channel surfing, I saw a silver pendant on one of the home shopping channels. I thought the pendant was really ugly, but I kept watching. Why? Who knows? Probably sheer inertia.

Still, I listened to the hostess describe the piece. She went on and on about the unusual shape, the intricate carved work on the pendant, and the way it caught the light. Before long, I found myself thinking about buying the pendant.

Thankfully, I came to my senses before I ordered it. With more than a little embarrassment, I realized the hostess had practically talked me into buying something I didn't like. How did she do it? By focusing on the positive.

Positive thinking isn't something new. The concept has been around forever. Maybe that's because there's something to it. Positive thinking is the key to being confident.

Think about those days when you wake up with a pimple on the end of your nose or a cold sore the size of a walnut on your lip. On those days, if you're like most people, you go out into the world with at least part of your mind focused on that big flaw. In doing so, you're calling attention to the negative. How many silver pendants do you think the shopping channels would sell if they said something like "Well, I know the shape of this thing is a little odd, but . . ."

You project out into the world whatever it is that you focus on. What do you think happens when you go out thinking, *I hope people don't notice my pimple?* You are, in effect, focusing your attention on the flaw, which magnetizes people's attention to it as well.

If you sold yourself the way the shopping channels sell their products, you'd present a whole different picture to the world. So you feel your age is showing in sagging skin or more wrinkles than you'd like. You could be thinking, *I've got great legs.* If you don't have such great legs, you could be thinking, *I have lovely hands.* If you're math-challenged, you could be thinking, *I have great interpersonal skills.*

See how it works. Focus on the positive. Own who you are and what you have to offer. Put your attention on your strengths. Remind yourself of what you're good at. Tell yourself that you can learn to accomplish whatever you're not good at, if you want to. Give yourself credit for the highlights of you instead of lamenting the downsides of you. Shine a spotlight on yourself that will seek out everything about you that you approve of. Then, talk it up. Tell yourself how great you are at this or that and how wonderful certain aspects of your personality or body are.

When you keep your attention on what you do well, on what you like about yourself, you will be confident. Whenever you notice a fault or make a mistake, acknowledge it, accept it, and then return your attention to your strengths. Also, work to develop more strengths, more things you like about yourself. Use your challenges to create confidence. Whenever you triumph, add the success to your confidence quotient.

If you want to see how this is done, turn on a TV shopping channel. Just be careful you don't end up with a vacuum cleaner you don't need.

∽ BECOMING CONFIDENT

Day 1: Ask to be confident.

Day 2: Affirm your desire to become confident.

Day 3: Act as if you're confident.

Day 4: List your strengths, both inner and outer. Write down everything you like about yourself. Read the list several times.

Day 5: Gather a group of friends willing to help each other build confidence. Now, together, create "I am" boxes. For each friend, write at least ten things you like about him or her on ten separate pieces of paper. Your friends will do the same for you and for all the others in the group. Buy or make a small decorative box and put into it all the pieces of paper your friends give you. Have each person in the group do the same thing with their pieces of paper. Take your box home. Frequently take the papers out of your box and use them to fill in the blank in this sentence: "I am _____." In other words, if a friend has written "smart," say "I am smart."

Day 6: Before you head out today, pick something about yourself that you like. Talk about it as you drive to work, to the store, or wherever. For instance, say "I have a great smile. It's such a real, genuine smile. It's infectious. It makes other people smile." Talk yourself up. It will keep you focused on the positive aspects of yourself.

Day 7: If you're having a bad hair day or if you make a mistake, say to yourself, *Yes, okay, my hair looks awful* (or *I messed up* or whatever), *but I'm* _____. Fill in the blank with one of your positive qualities. Refocus on the positive.

Courageous

Courageous leads the forces onto the battlefield. It wears a flashy helmet and a suit of bright, silver armor. It is undaunted by obstacles. It is a banner of possibility. It hears doubts and fears whispering, grumbling, and screaming, but it pays no heed to the babbling sound. Courageous tries new things. When it falls, it gets up and tries more new things. Courageous is being in fear but being in action at the same time.

IN YEARS PAST, I LOST COUNT OF THE NUMBER OF TIMES well-meaning friends told me I would never find the man of my dreams if I insisted on living a solitary life and refused to join clubs or go to social events to meet people. I would end up alone forever, these people said, if I didn't live my life differently. These people thought I lacked courage because I refused to get out into the world in the way they thought was necessary.

For me, however, being courageous required that I remain true to myself. I expected the love of my life to come at the time and place that was a natural fit with my living just the way I needed to live. I was saying yes to living *my* authentic

life instead of saying no to living that life and being someone I wasn't just so I could meet a man.

Taped above my computer screen is the question "What
would you do if you knew you couldn't fail?" This is my daily
challenge: doing those things that terrify me. They terrify
me because I'm afraid I *will* fail. So to do them, I have to tell
myself I *cannot* fail. And so I cannot, because it is the doing
that is the triumph. This is being courageous. Being courageous is saying yes to opportunity instead of saying no.

The courageous person is the one who jumps out first,
who goes after that which appears unattainable. You must
be willing to be a step ahead if you want to be courageous.
You might have to pave the way for yourself and for those
who follow you.

When you're courageous, you look failure and danger in
the face and act anyway. It doesn't matter what you're trying
to accomplish. Most of what you do will require courage.
Most of what you do, at least that which truly matters, will
be a leap into the unknown.

Being courageous requires taking risks, being willing to
do something that just might fail. To be courageous, you
must shed your self-consciousness because you might have
to look stupid or silly to get what you want. If you're doing
something no one else has done, you might get judged,
laughed at, or criticized. If you want to reach your goal, you
need to be willing to face the derisive voices of those who
don't understand your passion.

Being courageous is the ability to withstand the on-
slaught of opinion that tells you what you're doing isn't
going to work. It's knowing what you want and attempting to

get it, even when the odds are long and the way is hard. It is that leap into the dark. It is acting even when you would much rather curl up into a ball and safely munch your way through a package of Oreos. In some situations, like waiting for the right person to come along at the right time, the action will be quiet action, such as trusting and expecting. Even doing nothing can be a courageous action. Being courageous is simply knowing what needs to be done and boldly doing it.

Most of the courage you hear about in the news has to do with heroic acts that save lives or daredevil attempts to set some kind of record. This is grand courage, the kind that comes with fanfare and gets all the attention. But the kind of courage you need to live a quality life is the quiet kind, the kind that will get you out of bed in the morning to go to that job interview. This kind of courage will help you start a business, go back to school, or sign up and train for a marathon, even though you've never run one before. Quiet courage will help you raise your kids and love your spouse.

What would you try to do if you knew you could not fail? Whatever it is, be courageous and do it.

ᴄ Becoming Courageous

Day 1: Ask to be courageous.

Day 2: Affirm your desire to become courageous.

Day 3: Act as if you're courageous.

Day 4: Write down the things you'd do if you knew you couldn't fail. What do you want to try that you haven't tried because of fear?

Day 5: Write "YES!" on several Post-it notes and place them all over your home. They will remind you to say yes to possibility and opportunity instead of saying no.

Day 6: Choose something you really want that you're afraid to go after (something from the list you made on day 4). Now imagine what it will be like to get that thing or do it, whatever it is. Really feel it. Get yourself out of feeling fear about it and feel triumph instead. This will help you get in a mind-set to take courageous action.

Day 7: Just as in "Adventurous," pick one of the things you want but are afraid to go after, and take just one small step toward it today. Again, even making a list of action steps is a step. Or make a phone call to get information or buy a book about what you want. One step creates quiet courage.

Creative

Creative flies freely on gentle breezes, soars proudly on strong winds, and rests contentedly in soft rain. Creative is open and willing. Creative makes things, things that bear the stamp of self. It is strong and brave. It looks for possibilities where others see nothing. Creative lives outside the expected and is quite comfortable there.

MY FRIEND JACKIE LIVES A RICH, CREATIVE LIFE. HER CREATIVITY is obvious in her appearance, in her work as a massage therapist, and in her interaction with people. And you should have seen the beautiful wedding cake she made for my husband and me when we got married.

"It's just a little hobby," Jackie said when we raved about the cake.

Jackie also carves free-form sculptures from pieces of driftwood.

"Oh, it's just something I do," she said when I complimented her on them.

She regularly dismisses her obvious creative talent. Jackie has even asserted, "Oh, I'm not creative."

When I first heard her say that about herself, I was shocked, and I protested, "But you are."

"Do you really think so?" Jackie asked. "I've never thought of myself as creative."

Are you like Jackie? Do you not realize how creative you are?

Creativity is an aspect of almost everything you do. It certainly plays a part in the way you dress, how you decorate your home, how you cook a meal, or how you do your work.

Creativity is bringing life and passion to your actions. It is doing tasks with a bit of flair, with the touch of your own uniqueness. You can turn almost anything into a creative act. You simply need to approach your task with mindfulness and a bit of enthusiasm and zest. If you live your life this way, you can be creative with whatever you're doing.

You don't have to be a poet, dancer, or actor to be creative. Some people are creative mothers. Some are creative pet owners. Some are creative small business owners. Anyone can live a creative life.

To live a creative life, you need to nurture your creative spirit. To do this, you must redefine creativity. You need to look for creativity in even the most mundane places. If you apply creativity to the normal banalities of life, it will spark the spirit of play that will spur you into more and more creative thought.

Creativity is about looking at the world in new ways. For example, novelist Isabel Allende says, "When I see a gadget, say a blender, I imagine how I can use it for something else. I'm always trying to get things to do what they're not supposed to do."[3] She believes creativity is looking for the unique in all that you encounter.

Some people who create for a living have a tendency to turn creativity into something difficult, something elusive, even something to be feared. As a writer, I know I have often viewed creativity as a wild thing I need to corral and control so I can use it for my own advantage. When it gets away from me, I feel cheated and deprived. I am bereft. I can't write. I think creativity has abandoned me altogether.

But when I think that way, I'm wrong. Creativity never leaves me. It's always there for me to use. I just have to choose how to use it.

Creativity has the capacity to turn the treadmill of life into a playground. Everything you do can be approached as drudgery or as a possibility to create something fresh, new, and exciting. If you go through your day letting your creative spirit lead the way, you will find joy in all you do.

৩ BECOMING CREATIVE

Day 1: Ask to be creative.

Day 2: Affirm your desire to become creative.

Day 3: Act as if you're creative.

Day 4: Celebrate your creativity. List the things you do that are creative—things you do with enthusiasm and unique flair. You'll probably be surprised at how long your list is. Pat yourself on the back for all the ways you are creative.

Day 5: Look for ways to be even more creative. Pick something you need to do and do it just a little differently than the way you usually do it.

Day 6: Play with your food at least once today. Before you eat your salad, make a pretty design with the vegetables. Before you eat dinner, build a tower, a river, or a star out of your food. Have fun with this. The idea is to bring creativity into something mundane. It will remind you to be creative in all your activities.

Day 7: Today create something more concrete. It doesn't have to be anything huge. Maybe write a two-line poem or make up a new silly tune to hum. Cook something without following a recipe. Make a paper airplane. Draw a picture. Take a photograph. Teach your dog a new trick. Don't make this difficult. You don't need to write a novel or a symphony. Just do some little creative thing. Notice how good it makes you feel.

Determined

Determined lets no one stop it. Other people's opinions are like a mist falling on the path ahead. Doubt is like a gnat brushed aside by a strong hand. Determined climbs right over obstacles and keeps going. It looks for shortcuts but doesn't mind when it has to go the long way. Determined never gives up, and it always reaches its destination.

IN EARLY 2002, MY BELOVED SPRINGER SPANIEL, MUGGINS, who was ten years old at the time, became severely ill. Her struggles began in April with a bout of severe vomiting. She was hospitalized and diagnosed with pancreatitis. The veterinarian told me pancreatitis could be successfully treated, but it could also be fatal.

I decided that, for Muggins, the disease would not be fatal. Muggins is the canine love of my life. She brightens my days. She fills me with delight. I am passionate about Muggins living a long, happy life. I wanted Muggins to get better. So I made the decision to do what was necessary to heal her, and I resolved to make it happen.

My quest to reach the goal of Muggins's good health took me in many directions, required many resources, both monetary and personal, and demanded creative and open-minded thinking. It led me to several veterinarians, energy healers, an animal communicator, an animal acupuncture therapist, and a nutritionist. This path eventually led to a different diagnosis, the correct one. An internal veterinary medicine specialist conducted several pricey tests that revealed Muggins has inflammatory bowel disease. The pancreatitis was a secondary problem, not the real cause of her symptoms.

Once I received the correct diagnosis, I was able to pursue new avenues of information and action. I perused books and Web sites. I became familiar with herbs and supplements available at health food stores. I learned new skills, like creating healthy home-cooked meals for animals. Along the way, my efforts to heal Muggins encouraged me to nurture many of my inner qualities too, qualities like patience, gratitude, purpose, and strength. My determination to heal Muggins took me on quite an adventure. It's an adventure that, as I write this, is still ongoing.

This is how determination works. You make a decision, one born of some goal that matters very much to you, and you find inner resolve. That resolve is the belief that you can get what you want and the hope that your efforts will be enough for what it takes to achieve success. Decision and resolve make determination.

Being determined is an instructive quality. When you are determined, you often learn a lot about yourself and the world along the way to your destination. You also learn new skills. Your resolve takes you into new territories in your life.

Being determined is also a fertilizer for other qualities. It forces the use of qualities such as being creative and open-minded. It also nourishes many qualities, including being patient, persistent, and strong. Determination is like the railroad track to your destination. The other qualities you need to meet your resolve roll along on the back of being determined.

Sometimes, some of the best things in life, like the health of a loved one, only come to you if you're determined. Much of what you want in life—success, love, and joy—lies in a room behind a door that can only be opened with the key of determination.

Determination got you born. If you don't think your mother needed to be determined to get through pregnancy and birth, you're wrong. Determination got you raised. Only a determined person can parent a child to adulthood. And now that you are an adult, being determined will get you a full life.

ꙅ Becoming Determined

Day 1: Ask to be determined.

Day 2: Affirm your desire to become determined.

Day 3: Act as if you're determined.

Day 4: Think back to a time in your life when you had to be determined to get what you wanted. Maybe you've had such an experience recently. Maybe you were a kid the last time you were determined. Remember what you did and what it felt like. Familiarize yourself with what it feels like to be determined.

Day 5: Ask someone to tell you a story about how being determined got them what they wanted. The more you hear about determination in action, the more you will be inspired to act similarly.

Day 6: Think of something you really want, something you may have to work very hard to get. Write a simple contract for yourself. Describe what you want and write "I, [your name], am determined to achieve this goal. I will not give up until I have it." Sign the contract and date it. Refer to it whenever you feel like giving up on what you want.

Day 7: Stand up right now. Walk across the room. Look back to where you started. Remind yourself that you wouldn't have gotten across the room if you hadn't been determined to do so. Sure, this was easy, but being determined in all things works the same way no matter how complicated the task. Think of this little walk every time you need to be determined.

Disciplined

Disciplined knows how to stick to a plan. Disciplined brushes its teeth every day. It exercises and eats right. Disciplined is strong enough to carry other qualities, such as playful and adventurous. It can rest sometimes and let chaos reign, but it knows when to step in and restore order. Disciplined follows a recipe for life, and it never forgets an ingredient.

A FEW YEARS AGO, I SPENT THREE MONTHS ON A STRICT food regimen, consuming only whole or juiced raw fruits and vegetables. When I first began the program, my intention was to improve my health. I'd read that such a program could cleanse the body and remove toxins. Also, obviously, it would remove weight, and I very much needed to remove weight.

Those three months were exceedingly challenging. Each day, I had to get up and make fresh juice. Even when cereal or toast sounded so much better, I had to choose fruit instead. When I would pass a restaurant with the aromas of good, hot food wafting from it, I had to munch on my raw veggies or drink my carrot-spinach juice. I had to use my will to bypass what my pleasure centers were calling for.

Anyone who has been on a diet knows what I'm talking about.

After a week or so of doing this, I realized that there were far easier and healthier ways to detoxify my body and lose weight. It no longer seemed logical to me to do what I was doing, and I was tempted to give up the program. But by then, I'd begun to discover something rewarding about the process itself.

To do what I was doing, I had to practice enormous discipline. My ego mind (that part of my mind that's always chattering about what is and isn't right for me) was telling me that eating this diet was senseless and too much trouble for what it was worth, but I made myself follow the program just for the sake of following the program. I made myself keep going just for the practice of making myself keep going. In other words, I did it to practice discipline. I figured if I could assert my will to follow this eating program for three months, I could assert my will to do anything.

Now, I'm not advocating going on a fast or a strict fruit-and-vegetable diet. I'm not sure, in the long run, that that three-month eating experiment was the healthiest thing I've done for my physical body. I do know, though, that in doing it, I stumbled on to one of the best programs I've done for inner growth.

You see, during those three months, I discovered something quite extraordinary. While my ego mind was busy dealing with the details of the eating program, my wiser mind had more room to speak up. Consequently, during those three months, my intuition became stronger and I had more inner peace. After the three months were over,

I realized I was a stronger person because I knew I had the ability to do anything I set my mind to do, even if it was difficult or uncomfortable.

Being disciplined has two parts. First, it is a conduit for focusing the mind to get clarity in all aspects of your life. But more than that, it is direct access to a healthy, happy life. Discipline is like a fence around your behavior, and fences can set helpful boundaries.

For example, my dog, Muggins, has a fenced backyard. But rather than limit her pleasure, the fence enhances it. Because she has a fence, she doesn't have to be tied up. She can go outside anytime she wants when I'm home, and the fence allows her to romp in a wooded canine playground safe from cars and other things that might hurt her. She delights in her yard and enjoys hours of fun in it.

Being disciplined isn't a cage that prevents you from having fun. It's a boundary that gives you a safe, healthy place within which to roam.

I use discipline to stay mentally healthy. I'm bipolar, which means I'm prone to sinking into long periods of depression alternating with periods of hyperenergy. In order to avoid the havoc these mood swings have wreaked in my life, I have developed a set of behaviors that help me stay on an even keel. Doing these behaviors requires discipline. I exercise every day. I meditate. I take a combination of herbs and supplements that keeps me feeling good. I do not always want to do these things. But I know they make me feel the way I want to feel, so I exercise my will and choose to do them for my own best self. That's discipline.

Discipline isn't about punishment or deprivation. It's

about reward and abundance. Creating a structure in your life does nothing to take away from your life. On the contrary, it adds to it.

❧ BECOMING DISCIPLINED

Day 1: Ask to be disciplined.

Day 2: Affirm your desire to become disciplined.

Day 3: Act as if you're disciplined.

Day 4: Make a list of habitual choices you make that are bad for you. Write at the bottom of the list "These choices are NOT an option." Put this someplace where you will see it often.

Day 5: What do you need to do to be healthy? Today make a list of actions you need to take, such as brush your teeth, eat vegetables, exercise, and so on. Create a chart listing these things. Make a square for each day. Buy some gold stars or get a bright colored pen to draw stars. Check off items on your list as you do them and give yourself a star if you do more than half the things on your list. (You're not going for perfection here—you're just getting used to some structure.)

Day 6: What do you need to do to be successful at your work? Make a similar chart for your work actions, at least the ones you have trouble getting yourself to do. Check off items on your list as you do them and reward yourself with a star.

Day 7: Make a list and chart for your spiritual and emotional life, including relationships. What do you need to do to feel good? My list has things such as ask for guidance, hug and cuddle my husband and dog, accept what is, and expect the best outcome. Again, make a chart and check off what you do. Reward yourself with a star.

Faithful

Faithful wears a hat of sureness and a cloak of belief. It sings a tune of expectation and recites words of trust. Faithful walks blindly into a room and knows that it will find its way around. It jumps off cliffs and expects to be able to fly. It sets off across wide oceans and knows that its boat will be seaworthy and that it will weather all storms. Faithful knows tomorrow will always come.

SEVERAL YEARS AGO, A FRIEND AND I TOOK A SELF-DEFENSE class that also taught self-empowerment. To get us to the point where we could stand strong and confident, the class instructors had us participate in many exercises designed to make us aware of our own power. One of those exercises required us to climb to the top of a six-foot ladder and fall back into the waiting arms of our two dozen classmates. The exercise was called "Leap of Faith."

I thought the exercise was a blast, and I had no trouble falling backward into the arms of the other women. My friend, however, found the task daunting.

She was able to climb the ladder with no problem. Once she got there, however, she couldn't bring herself to fall back. The instructors tried to encourage her. They coaxed her. They reassured her. So did the other women and I, but my friend simply couldn't seem to do it. Finally the instructors allowed my friend to come down a step and, instead of falling, sort of sit down onto the outstretched arms of the women waiting to catch her. Afterward my friend told me that for her, the exercise wasn't so much a "Leap of Faith" as it was a "Squat of Little Faith."

This friend is usually not a fearful woman, so I think she just had an off day. Or maybe she had a magnificent day, one that brought her face-to-face with a fear she needed to conquer. That's part of developing faith—facing your fears and conquering them.

Being faithful is about courage and facing fears, but it's more that that. It's about trust. To be faithful means to have a knowing about something, an expectation. It's more than hope. It's something akin to having an intention. Being faithful is believing in something, be it yourself, your dream, a divine being, or a particular outcome.

Although I have no trouble falling backward off a ladder into the arms of others, I do have trouble with faith in other parts of my life. In the money arena, for example, I am full of doubt.

Doubt is the opposite of faith. It is the enemy of faith. So is being fearful. If faithful is a boat that sails across the sea, doubtful is a small hole that lets in water. Fearful is a jagged gash in the hull that sinks the boat in a manner of minutes.

When it comes to money, for years my faithful boat had trouble getting even a few feet from shore. I was so filled with fear that faith didn't have a chance. When it came to money, I could relate to my friend's "Squat of Little Faith."

The thing is, though, that life continued to reassure me, just like the other women did for my friend. It showed me, over and over, that I had nothing to fear. Money has come my way from unexpected sources, and that money allowed me to keep doing what I love to do. Because of these events, little by little, I've been able to re-route my thoughts to avoid the rocks of negativity and fear that gash into my faithful boat.

Of course I sometimes lack faith in other parts of my life, but seeing how all has worked out with money helps me have faith where I haven't yet seen things work out. Being faithful in one area of your life can help you be faithful in another.

A true and strong faith in a divine being, for example, will give you faith in everything. Faith in yourself can give you faith in others and vice versa. Faith in your dream can give you faith in your health. Being faithful begets being faithful.

Need a jump start on being faithful? Try rejoicing. When you can disconnect from your doubts and fears and rejoice in the moment, you pull faith into your life. The ability to enjoy what is has a way of creating an expectation for a positive future.

If rejoicing doesn't work, try "squatting." If you can't leap into the unknown, don't let that stop you from moving into the unknown slowly and gently. If you need to squat, squat. Just don't stay on the ladder. The ladder is a place of doubt and fear. The universe, which is waiting to catch you when you act, is the place of faith. It is there that you will find a knowing. You will know that all is well.

☡ BECOMING FAITHFUL

Day 1: Ask to be faithful.

Day 2: Affirm your desire to become faithful.

Day 3: Act as if you're faithful.

Day 4: What are you afraid of? Write down your fears. Then tear them up. This is a symbolic act that will free you to be faithful.

Day 5: Think of a time in your life when you were afraid but you kept going anyway. You kept doing what you needed to do and everything worked out. Remind yourself that fear falls away in the face of faith.

Day 6: Pray daily. Ask for what you need. Expect to get it. Practice being faithful to a divine being.

Day 7: Make a "God box." Get a small box. Write down your problems on little pieces of paper and put them in the box—give the problem to God or to whatever divine being you believe in. Expect solutions to come when the time is right.

Forgiving

Forgiving knows how to let go. It may not like what happened, but it won't linger over it. Forgiving carries no baggage. It accepts what is and releases the rest. It knows how to say "It's done." Forgiving knows when the past is over. It is a handshake and a hug that invites the new and says good-bye to the old.

IN JUNE 1972, PHAN THI KIM PHUC WAS SCORCHED BY NApalm that was dropped on her village in Vietnam. The image of her suffering was captured in a Pulitzer Prize–winning photo of Kim, who was stark naked and crying, fleeing the village along with other children after the attack.

John Plummer was the pilot and officer who ordered and carried out the attack, and after he saw the photograph of Kim, he was devastated. Tormented by guilt for more than twenty-four years, he lived with recurrent nightmares about the incident.

In 1996, Kim, who made it through the seventeen operations she needed and then created a good life for herself, despite the scars and pain she carried with her from childhood, spoke one day at a Veteran's Day observance in Washington, D.C. Plummer went to listen to her. When Kim said in her speech that "we cannot change history, but we should try to do good things for the present," Plummer decided to identify himself to her. When he did, she hugged him.

Plummer, sobbing, said to her, "I'm so sorry. I'm just so sorry."

Kim said, "It's all right. I forgive. I forgive."[4]

For some reason, most people like to carry around invisible bags of pain. They love gathering up old hurts and tucking them in next to disappointments in a huge suitcase of anger, bitterness, and resentment they lug around every day of their lives.

And what's wrong with that, you may ask? When people do horrible things, why should you forgive them? If they touch your life in some substantive, negative way you can never completely erase, don't you have the right to hate them for it?

Of course you do. Kim certainly had a right to hate Plummer. No one would have blamed her if she'd hauled around a trunk-sized suitcase of rage directed at the man who gave her a lifetime of pain. So why didn't she do that? She obviously made a choice to embrace the present and let go of what happened to her years before. What would hanging on to her anger have done for her anyway? Would it have made her pain go away? Would it have given her a better life?

Of course not.

When you define yourself by your old hurts, you limit your life. How can you possibly have a joyful life full of the freedom to choose activities and people who fill you with laughter and light if you're weighted down by the injustice of what was done to you years before?

Keep in mind that when you forgive someone, you are not saying you approve of or are in any way okay with what the person did. You aren't condoning child abuse, for instance, if you forgive the abuser. Forgiveness doesn't embrace the act. It embraces the person who committed the act—you accept that person as a flawed human being who screwed up. Forgiveness is a conscious decision to choose present joy rather than past pain.

This kind of forgiveness is possible with the people in your life—and with yourself. When you mess up big time, you can go around kicking yourself over it for days, months, or years, or you can choose to accept that you messed up and put the pain behind you. Instead of beating yourself up, you're choosing to lighten your emotional load so you can more easily lift yourself up.

Being forgiving is leaving the past in the past. To do this, you need to make a conscious decision to let go in every situation that hurts you or angers you in some way. I find it useful to do this aloud, but you can do it silently. I ask myself whether I really want to take this pain with me into the rest of my life. The answer to that question, of course, is no. I ask whether it will do me any good to continue to be angry, resentful, or hateful. Again, the answer is no. Then I tell myself, *Let it go.*

My husband, Tim, puts it this way. "I don't like being angry and resentful, so I choose not to be." Being forgiving, then, is a choice. It is the ability to set down your heavy bags of pain and travel lightly into the future possibilities of your life. If you want this freedom, you need to learn to say and truly mean "I forgive. I forgive."

ᴝ Becoming Forgiving

Day 1: Ask to be forgiving.

Day 2: Affirm your desire to become forgiving.

Day 3: Act as if you're forgiving.

Day 4: Make a list of people you need to forgive (include yourself, if necessary). Now pick the person you need to forgive the most and write "I forgive [name of person]" ten times. This may seem silly, but it tends to create an energy shift that makes room for forgiveness.

Day 5: If you've been holding a longtime grudge, write a letter of forgiveness to the person or people against whom you hold the grudge. Put the letter aside for a couple days, then read it over. If you feel like your energy has shifted and you can let the grudge go, tear up the letter. If you feel like you need to send the letter, do so after you're sure you've worded it in a way that won't create future regrets.

Day 6: Ask yourself whether you define yourself by an old hurt. For example, do you think of yourself as a "wronged person" because your spouse cheated or are you an "abused person" because your lover beat you up? Certainly these descriptions do describe you if you've had these experiences, but do you want them to *define* you? Consider redefining yourself, that is, thinking of yourself in a way that doesn't include the old hurt. For instance, you could be a "creative person" who at one time experienced abuse. The abuse was an experience. It isn't who you are.

Day 7: Imagine the rest of your life and what you want to accomplish and have in it. Will your angers, resentments, and hurts help you get what you want? If not, write them down and tear them up. Let them go. They are stopping you from getting what you truly want in life.

Free

Free is a wild horse, untethered from daily responsibility and worry. Free responds to necessity but not false obligation. Free faces each day with joy because it knows no addiction or compulsion. It carries no guilt or hatred. It moves with the confidence of its boundless possibility and flies over the chasms of negativity. Free runs. Or it doesn't. It is open to choose.

MY DOG, MUGGINS, SAYS A FRIEND OF MINE, IS LIKE AN orca whale because of the similarity of Muggins's tail to the whale's dorsal fin. When an orca is in captivity, its dorsal fin is not upright. It droops over to one side, limp and defeated. When an orca is free to roam in the ocean depths, its dorsal fin is erect and clearly signals the whale's triumphant freedom.

When Muggins is on a leash, her little stub of a tail with its white feathery fur hangs down, limp. But when she's off her leash, free to run and explore in a wooded park or on a vast beach, her tail is erect and the flutter of that white fur signals her triumphant freedom. Just like an orca whale.

Muggins loves to be free. She doesn't mind boundaries, such as the six-foot fence that surrounds her large, wooded yard or the calling distance I require her to be within when we're on the beach. But she abhors being confined in a way that gives her no space to explore and be herself.

Muggins isn't the only one who needs her freedom. I need it too. So do you.

Unlike for Muggins, orca whales, and other critters, being free is a choice for you and me. It is something we can do for ourselves.

Few of us, unless we commit a crime or are in some truly unusual situation, will be physically confined. Sure, we'll sometimes find ourselves in places we don't want to be. When I was in college, for example, I often felt like I was in captivity during some of my classes. Law school classes certainly seemed like jail cells much of the time.

But the truth is that these classes and other experiences I've had, like some jobs I've held, felt like confinement because they weren't choices I'd made willingly and wholeheartedly. These were activities I engaged in because I thought I had to or because I felt obligated. When I was in classes I was passionate about and when I held jobs I enjoyed, I never felt like I was in jail. Why? Because I enthusiastically chose the situations I was in.

That's freedom. Being free is the ability to know yourself well enough to be aware of what you like and don't like, what you want and don't want, and what you are willing or unwilling to do. It is the embracing of a goal and everything that goes along with attaining that goal. It is being conscious of everything you do in your life and, to the best of your ability, doing only what you believe in fully.

Doing things you don't want to do is like being on a leash when you want to be running loose or being in an aquarium when you'd much rather be in the ocean. You tether yourself when you fill your life with activities that stem from obligation.

In the true sense of the word, being free is being without restriction, being unconfined. Of course, in the real world, this isn't possible. Life, by necessity, comes with restrictions. Society builds boundaries around you, not unlike the boundaries Muggins must accept. You may not have to live inside a fenced yard or stay within earshot of a specific person, but if you want to find your way in the world, you do have to live inside certain social constructs and stay within earshot of the world's expectations for acceptable behavior.

Yet within these loose guidelines, you can be free. The truth is that it's not society that generally takes away your freedom—it's you.

You put restrictions on yourself. You may have learned those restrictions from society, say from a magazine or a TV show, or you may have learned them from your family, say from a parent. But by the time you're an adult, you're the one perpetuating those restrictions.

If you want to go around with your tail upright and wagging, you need to get to know yourself. Let go of the restrictions you've placed on yourself. Choose your own standards instead of someone else's standards. Live in a way that makes sense for you. Be free.

ꙅ BECOMING FREE

Day 1: Ask to be free.

Day 2: Affirm your desire to become free.

Day 3: Act as if you're free.

Day 4: Notice the things you do that feel like prisons or confinement. Ask yourself whether you do these things because you have to. If so, begin thinking about ways you could change your life to be free of obligations that don't suit you.

Day 5: Describe your perfect day. What would you be doing each day if you lived a life of freedom, one that suited you exactly? You need to know what being free means to you before you can be free.

Day 6: Check all your standards, such as those of behavior, appearance, and success. Are they yours or someone else's, like your parents' or spouse's? If they're not yours, consider changing them.

Day 7: Imagine that you have a tail. What would make it wag? Do more tail-wagging things.

Fun-Loving

Fun-loving is a whirling dance on the beach. It is a giggle in a quiet room. Fun-loving is open to possibility. Fun-loving finds enjoyment in anything that could be fun. Fun-loving doesn't mind being alone. It doesn't search for its entertainment. It expects it. And then fun-loving becomes it, with a bouncing leap of glee.

WHEN MY HUSBAND, TIM, AND I FIRST GOT TOGETHER, IT was across a great distance—from one side of the country to the other. Therefore, much of our early communication took place in cyberspace. We spent a lot of time in a private chat room where we could "talk" for hours without worrying about the cost of long-distance phone calls.

One night in our favorite chat room, we were discussing Tim's relationship with his then six-year-old daughter. He was telling me about the time he spent reading to her. Being a huge Winnie-the-Pooh fan, I asked him whether he read Pooh books to his daughter. "Oh yes," he responded. He said he really liked the character Tigger. I then typed a couple lines of a song about Tigger from a Winnie-the-Pooh movie.

Tim, to my delight, responded quickly: "T-I-double G-RRRRR."

I was smitten. Totally head over heels in love.

A couple days later when I told a friend about this new relationship, I said, "He got me with Tigger."

At first, my friend didn't get it, but when I told her the story, she did. She understood that I was so loopy for this man because he was clearly fun-loving.

Sometimes having fun will come your way easily. If you have a dog, for example, it's pretty much impossible to go through a day without fun. Dogs are all about fun. When you're annoyed because the toaster oven quit working or because the credit-card bill is bigger than you'd thought it would be, your dog will trot in with some silly toy hanging out of its mouth and wag the annoyance right out of your mind.

Kids are good for fun too. They can turn an ordinary task like making dinner into a recipe for giggles, if you allow them to. They can find fun things to do with mashed potatoes, Jell-O, and even boring old green beans.

But even though this kind of fun might be right in front of you, you won't enjoy it if you're not fun-loving.

I am so thankful Tim is fun-loving. He appreciates my silliness. When I buy him doofy stuffed animals that sing little songs or make funky noises, he smiles and says with obvious appreciation, "You're so fun." When I get the giggles over some stupid pun I've made, he says fondly, "You're so fun." And when I suggest we make love in the woods when we're on a hike and no one's around, he says with grateful excitement, "You are *so* fun." Yeah, I'm fun. The reason I'm fun is because I'm fun-loving.

Fun is the salt and pepper in a day. Without it, life lacks spice. Face it—life can be drudgery sometimes. Cleaning toilets, vacuuming out the car, and washing windows is pretty mundane stuff. But it doesn't have to be. Every one of those tasks, and most others, can be fun if you look for ways to make them fun. One of my favorite ways to have fun doing chores like these is to crank up the stereo and sing along, with high-volume enthusiasm, to as many songs as I know the words to, and many of those I don't. Making up songs about what I'm doing can be entertaining too.

All it takes to be fun-loving is a willingness to look for fun and enjoy it in whatever form it comes. If you can do that, you'll find that being fun-loving will raise the quality of your life to new heights.

∽ Becoming Fun-Loving

Day 1: Ask to be fun-loving.

Day 2: Affirm your desire to become fun-loving.

Day 3: Act as if you're fun-loving.

Day 4: Okay, you may have already done this in "Childlike," but do it again. Buy yourself a toy, something that will be purely fun.

Day 5: If you have a pet or a child, play with him or her today. If you don't have a pet or a child, find one to play with (in a *legal* and responsible way, like visiting a friend who has kids or pets).

Day 6: Make up a song about something you don't like doing, a song about going to work or about cleaning toilets or whatever. Sing it until you smile or, better yet, until you laugh.

Day 7: If you're doing something boring or unpleasant, stop a moment and think about how you could make it fun. For example, if you're peeling potatoes, pretend you're giving the potato a haircut. Talk to it and tell it how good it's going to look with a shaved head. Be silly.

Generous

Generous is a very small child with a mushy peanut-butter-and-jelly sandwich. It likes to toddle up to other people and offer them a bite. Generous believes in abundance, and it knows there is enough for everyone. It is just as happy giving as it is receiving, and it enjoys seeing others getting what they want as much as it enjoys getting what it wants. Generous is like the big blue sky. Its very existence touches others in a warm and wonderful way.

AFTER EDUARDO WITHDREW $4,000 FROM HIS BANK TO pay his employees, he and his two friends stopped at a store along a highway. While they were there, somehow the money fluttered out of the bank envelope and out the truck window.

Not long after that, a local trooper received a call about money in the roadway. He arrived to find several cars pulled off onto the shoulder of the highway while the cars' occupants dodged other speeding cars to try and grab the money.[5]

Eduardo and his friends, scrambling along with the grabby motorists to pick up $100s, $50s, and $20s, managed to retrieve $1,600. While most motorists stole the money they grabbed, one motorist picked up $1,200, which he returned to Eduardo. This man was the one generous person Eduardo encountered when he lost his cash. Yes, the man was also honest and had integrity, but in order to do what he did, he had to be generous.

When you hear the word *generous*, situations like this one, involving money, usually come to mind. Everyone likes it when someone is generous with money. But being generous with money isn't the only way to be generous. You can be poor and destitute and still be generous. Being generous isn't just about giving away money. It's simply about giving.

Life provides multiple opportunities to be generous in simple ways that don't require much effort. The low effort requirement, however, in no way lowers the positive effect of the generosity. When you're standing in line at the grocery store with a basket full of food and someone comes up behind you with only a couple items, you can be generous by allowing him or her to go ahead of you. If your neighbor needs to go to the doctor and her car isn't working, you can be generous and take her.

Generosity has a place in every part of your life. At work, you can be generous with your time and your effort. At home, you can be generous with your love and your caring.

Generosity, like kindness, starts with abundance. You give from an abundance within. If you are generous, you are like a full, boiling pot on the stove. You just naturally bubble over with giving.

Notice I said "naturally." Being generous is not the same as being responsible or meeting obligations. It doesn't come from "have to" or "need to." It comes from "want to." If a kindergarten teacher forces Billy to share his red crayon with Tommy, Billy, even if he gives the crayon to Tommy, is not generous. He is coerced. Only if Billy *wants* to give his crayon to Tommy is Billy being generous.

So how do you cultivate the quality of generosity? You remember how good it feels when someone gives you something you need or want, and you remember how good it feels when you give someone something they need or want and they shower you with thank-yous.

Generosity begins with awareness. If you notice what others are doing, you will unconsciously start looking for ways to help them do what they're doing. When you find a way to give that feels good to you, something you can do without it feeling like a strain or obligation, you will give with ease. That's generosity.

But generosity isn't necessarily just focused on others. You can be—in fact, you must be—generous with yourself as well. What can you give yourself? How about $20 to spend on a new book you don't really need but would like to have? That's self-generosity. How about a long, hot bath at the end of a hard day? That's self-generosity. If you're paying attention to yourself, you will notice what you need. Once you become generous, you will naturally give yourself what you need as much as you can.

If you have trouble cultivating generosity within yourself, watch others give. Watch kids. Watch your pets. Kids are generous with smiles and laughter. Dogs are generous with tail wags and licks. It doesn't matter what is given; the part that counts is what is received. When what you give generates joy and pleasure for you or someone else, you have been generous.

ꝏ Becoming Generous

Day 1: Ask to be generous.

Day 2: Affirm your desire to become generous.

Day 3: Act as if you're generous.

Day 4: Remember a time when you gave someone something that made him or her very happy. Linger over the good feelings you had.

Day 5: Notice what the people and animals around you are doing. Pick a person or animal and give him or her something that will help that person or animal in some way. (This doesn't have to be difficult. It can be as easy as opening a door for someone with his or her arms full.)

Day 6: Practice being generous with yourself. Give yourself something you want, be it a material item like a new CD or an experience like a long walk or a nap.

Day 7: Look for others being generous. See whether you can find ten ways people give to others today. These examples will give you ideas for your generous actions in the future.

Goal-Oriented

Goal-oriented never leaves home without knowing where it's going. Goal-oriented is visionary. It sees possibilities and figures out how to turn them into actualities. Goal-oriented has a plan and a result in mind. It enjoys the trip along the way, but ultimately, it wants to reach the viewpoint at the end of the trail.

WHEN I WAS A KID, I TOOK PIANO LESSONS. AT FIRST, I HAD to do piano exercises. This was just playing chords and notes to get the hang of the keys. If my teacher had forced me to stick with only the exercises, I bet my enthusiasm would have quickly gone flat. Instead, she had me play songs. This gave some direction to my playing, a goal to move toward. Instead of just making sound, I got to play music. Music is the goal of every instrument that's played, and all music starts with a vision.

Being goal-oriented also starts with a vision. A vision is a clear idea of where you'd like to be. It's a positive statement of something you want to accomplish. When I say a "positive statement," I mean that a vision is something you *want*, not something you *don't want*. "Don't wants" do not make good goals.

For example, I have a friend who has trouble keeping her house in order. She usually has so much clutter she panics when someone comes to her door because she doesn't want anyone to see "the mess."

"I don't know why I can't get a handle on this," my friend says. "I'm very organized at work. Why can't I be organized at home?"

Well, it's possible she's just not as motivated to be organized at home, but it's also possible she can't get what she wants because she doesn't have a clear idea of what she wants. She only knows she *doesn't want* the mess she lives with now. She doesn't have a clear vision in her mind of how she wants her house to look, of how she wants her belongings organized. Without a vision, a goal to move toward, all the action in the world will get you nowhere.

But a vision alone isn't enough either. Once you get a vision, you have to do something with it. You have to feed it.

In a story by an unknown author, a man said, "I feel as if I have two wolves fighting in my heart. One wolf is the vengeful, angry, violent one. The other wolf is the loving, compassionate one." When asked which wolf will win the fight, the man answered, "The one I feed."

The wolves in this man's heart are like the thoughts and ideas that pop into your head. Your thoughts and ideas will often be at odds with each other. Which ones will win? In other words, which ones will manifest themselves in your life? The ones you feed.

The way you feed ideas or thoughts is by creating a plan of action for them. Instead of letting the thoughts and ideas only exist in your mind as starving wolves with no place to go, you nourish them with your time, effort, and energy. You give them your attention.

If my friend, for instance, wants to clean up her house, she needs to set some concrete goals. Does she want her floor space to be free of clutter? Does she want to box up all her magazines? Does she want to put away all her clothes? Whatever it is she wants, she needs to see it as a vision and then take steps toward it. Each day, she needs to do some action that will feed her vision of a clean, organized house.

That's being goal-oriented.

But what about being spontaneous? What's wrong with that?

Nothing. Spontaneous is great too. But if you're *always* spontaneous, you may end up bouncing around like a ball in a pinball game that never strikes any bumpers and never scores.

Your days are a playing field and you have the ball. Are you going to run in circles with it or are you going to head toward a goal? It's your choice.

ᴐ BECOMING GOAL-ORIENTED

Day 1: Ask to be goal-oriented.

Day 2: Affirm your desire to become goal-oriented.

Day 3: Act as if you're goal-oriented.

Day 4: Write a list of goals. What do you want in your career and personal life? Write it down. This is the start of finding your vision.

Day 5: Take the goal from your list that calls to you the most and imagine what it will be like to have it. As I suggest in "Courageous," really feel what it will be like to have achieved that goal. That feeling is your vision.

Day 6: Now, with this goal in mind, write an action plan. How are you going to feed your goal? Write out the steps you need to take to reach it.

Day 7: Take a step toward the goal you've chosen or toward another goal. If one of your simple goals, for example, is to have a clean house, dust one room today. Or if one of your goals is to eliminate clutter, get rid of five things today. If you want to write a book, think up the title today. Baby steps will add up to eventually cover a lot of miles toward your goal.

Graceful

Graceful is a ballet dancer on stage. It is controlled and quiet, beautiful and flowing. Graceful allows. It uses its strengths to make the difficult look easy. Graceful moves from one place to the next without obvious effort. It breathes in peace and exhales satisfaction. Graceful is always loose and flexible. Graceful is a feather floating gently to the ground with perfect simplicity.

OKAY, I ADMIT IT. I'M PRONE TO TANTRUMS.

Apparently, I threw tantrums when I was a toddler, and my mom nipped the habit in the bud, punishing me when I tried kicking and screaming to express myself. So I quit with the tantrum thing for a while, but when I became an adult and there was no longer anyone to stop me from sharing my displeasure in a dramatic fashion, I returned to indulging in tantrums.

No, I didn't sit down in the middle of the aisle at the grocery store and wail and thrash around when I couldn't find my favorite brand of ice cream. My adult tantrums were of the more subtle variety, but they were still tantrums. They were an angry expression of resistance to things I didn't want to do.

For example, when my ex-husband and I had a house built many years ago, the contractor kept messing up. Every time he did, I'd rant and rave and demand that my ex-husband fix the situation. I complained to friends about how awful the home-building process was, and I even cried in frustration and rage.

Throwing tantrums is a negative way to experience life. Fortunately, there is another way to handle the challenges life brings your way: you can handle them with grace.

The word *graceful* usually evokes images of how people move. People who walk smoothly and fluidly are graceful. People who bump into walls and spill their coffee are not. But this isn't the kind of graceful I'm talking about.

My husband, Tim, although he's prone to knocking his head against cabinets and doorways and has an amazing capacity for finding things to trip over, is a great example of someone who is graceful. Tim does not throw tantrums. He simply handles whatever comes his way.

One day, for instance, the copy machine we have in our home office broke. Part of the piece that broke was a small spring. When Tim showed me what happened and asked me what I thought of his plan to fix it, I took the spring from him to look at it. I promptly dropped it, and it fell down into the workings of the copy machine and disappeared.

I cringed. "Oops."

Now, if Tim had done this and I was the one who had to fix the machine, I would have been ripe for a tantrum at that point. But Tim simply said, "It's okay. I'll get it out." He then spent the next half-hour holding the copy machine (which is not a lightweight thing, mind you) upside down, shaking it this way and that until he worked the spring loose and got it out. He never got angry. He never lamented the fact that he had to deal with a new problem. He just dealt with it. That's being graceful.

When you're graceful, you glide through your days. You may have to deal with a fender-bender, but you do so quietly and calmly. You may have to handle an irate co-worker, but you do so with charm and poise. You may have to handle a broken copy machine, but you do so with humor and optimism.

Being graceful about life means facing your challenges with calmness, poise, confidence, and determination. When you're graceful, you don't rage against the obstacles that are placed in your path. Instead, you acknowledge them and then figure out how to get around them. Being graceful, like being adaptable, requires that you accept the challenges you encounter.

Being graceful is a positive way of coping with the bumps in life's road. Instead of railing at the problems, you just accept them, find a way past them, and move on.

∽ BECOMING GRACEFUL

Day 1: Ask to be graceful.

Day 2: Affirm your desire to become graceful.

Day 3: Act as if you're graceful.

Day 4: Watch and see whether you throw tantrums. Do you react in a dramatic, negative way to problems or do you accept them? If you're a tantrum-thrower, own up to it.

Day 5: Think about three situations you've faced that looked like disasters but turned out okay. Remind yourself of these when you start to throw a tantrum about a new problem.

Day 6: Think about a tantrum you've thrown in the past. What blessings did you overlook while you whined and complained? For example, if you broke your ankle, did you overlook how nice it was to put your feet up and read a good book?

Day 7: When you face a challenge, practice saying, "It's okay. I'll do [whatever you need to do to solve the problem]." Even if you don't feel like it's okay, saying the words will help you practice actually *being* okay.

Grateful

Grateful looks at the world with eyes open to what is good. Grateful sees the joys and appreciates all the little things. It can relish a hamburger when it would rather have steak. It can see past a person's foibles and celebrate a person's attributes. Grateful listens for the soothing sounds and ignores the discordant notes. Grateful can always find something to love.

I LIVE IN A MODEST BUT COZY MODULAR HOME. MODULAR means that the house was built someplace else, then transported on flatbed trucks, in two sections, to its current location. When the house arrived, a crew of builders rolled the house halves off the flatbeds and onto a concrete footing foundation. Then they seamed the structure back together.

When the house arrived here, it was early February on the Washington coast. In other words, it was cold, in the low thirties, and the electricity wasn't turned on until the day after the house arrived. So the day it was put together, the inside of the house was about as cold as the outside.

My house is carpeted wall-to-wall. One of the crew's tasks when they set up the house was to stretch the carpet and tack it down. Ideally, carpet should be installed in a warm room because it will expand in heat. If stretched to its limit when cold, it will buckle once it warms.

The carpet in my house, now eight years after the house was seamed together, is lumpy and wrinkled in too many places to count. When the problem showed itself a few weeks after I moved in, I contacted the carpet installers. Although they sent someone out to re-stretch the carpet, he still wasn't able to smooth it out, and it got even worse during the following months and years.

I love my carpet. It's a tweedy blue color with flecks of beige, pale rose, and green. The flecks give the carpet a subdued muted look that disguises dirt and sand, a must when you have a dog and live in the forest near a beach. This carpet was the first one I'd ever chosen on my own, and I was proud of and quite pleased with my choice. For some time, it bugged the heck out of me that my beautiful carpet was marred by tacky wrinkles and buckles in almost every room.

But it doesn't bother me anymore. Why? Because now, instead of thinking about the carpet wrinkles, I think about how grateful I am for the color and plush comfort of the carpet. Instead of focusing on what's wrong, I'm giving thanks for what's right.

Dr. Christiane Northrup, an expert in creating great health, says you can improve your health by improving your attitude. She suggests you focus on what's right in your life, not on what's wrong. She advises, "Appreciate as much as you can about your life. Wallow in the good stuff."[6] In other words, be grateful.

Being grateful can be done in two little steps. One, look

around and find something that you like, something that makes you smile. Two, appreciate it. It's that simple.

So be grateful. Be grateful when you're cleaning toilets because you have toilets to clean. Be grateful when you're eating the same old peanut butter sandwich for lunch because you have something to eat. Be grateful for your job because it pays the rent. Be grateful when you're paying the bills because it means you have money to pay them. Be grateful for your family, your friends, and your guinea pig. Be grateful for your toes, your nose, and your little pinkie. If you can't sing, be grateful you can talk. If you can't dance, be grateful you can walk. If you can't walk, be grateful you can sit. If you can't sit, be grateful you can breathe.

I don't care how bad things get, you can always find something in your life that's good. Find the good. Practice gratitude and just see whether the bad things don't get a little bit better.

ᴥ Becoming Grateful

Day 1: Ask to be grateful.

Day 2: Affirm your desire to become grateful.

Day 3: Act as if you're grateful.

Day 4: Take some advice from Oprah Winfrey, who suggests keeping a gratitude journal. Write down at least three things you experienced today for which you're grateful. Do this every night from now on.

Day 5: As often as you can remember to do it today, stop and look around. Find something to like. Be grateful for it.

Day 6: Think of something that bugs you, like the bad alignment in your car or a leaky roof. Now find something about the situation to be happy about. For example, if your car pulls to the right, be happy you have a steering wheel to correct the problem. If your roof leaks, be happy it keeps out the majority of the rain.

Day 7: Take a deep breath. Smile and say, with feeling, "I'm grateful for breathing."

Honorable

Honorable is above reproach. It welcomes scrutiny because it knows it will shine in any light, no matter how bright. It invites the world to examine its actions, knowing those actions are all grounded in honesty and integrity. Honorable lives by a set of rules that take some effort to adhere to. It never takes the easy shortcut if that shortcut will trample the rules. Honorable is in it for the long haul.

WHEN I WAS SIX YEARS OLD, I SHOPLIFTED A BUBBLE GUM cigar. It was blue, my favorite color. It had that fun little gold band wrapped around it that made it look like a real cigar (if we forget, of course, that real cigars aren't blue). I slid the cigar, oh so easily, down the front of my underpants so I could take it home.

I don't remember chewing that bubble gum cigar, although I assume I did. I don't know whether it tasted good. I don't know whether it gave me any pleasure. What I do know is I've never forgotten that I stole it. I felt bad about it, so bad that I never forgot the bad feeling. It's the feeling you get when you've not acted with honor.

I'd like to say the bubble gum cigar was the only thing I

have ever stolen in my life, but that wouldn't be true. I have a really nice stapler on my desk that I purloined from an employer who made me mad. I justified it by telling myself I was never paid enough to begin with, I hadn't been treated well, and hey, it's only a stapler. What's the big deal?

I didn't act honorably. That's the big deal.

Being honorable requires strict adherence to ethical conduct. When you're honorable, you don't blur the lines. You don't find ways to break the rules because you want something and the ethical rules prevent you from having it.

Being honorable holds up all your other actions. If you don't have a solid framework of honor, the "house" of your life can, and probably will at some point, crumble down around your shoulders.

Honor, however, isn't an easy quality to cultivate. It's meticulous in its demands on your behavior. It requires that you do more than adhere to legal and societal rules. It requires that you examine every situation you encounter and do your best to act ethically.

One way to know you're not acting honorably is when you make excuses for your actions, when you try to justify what you're doing so you feel okay about it. When a nagging voice within is telling you that what you're doing is wrong, then what you're doing *is* wrong.

I have, I'm sorry to say, done several dishonorable things in my life, things of which I'm not proud. The bubble gum cigar and the stapler excepted, I don't go around stealing things. But honor is about more than not stealing. Honor requires that you tell people the truth. It requires that you treat people fairly. It demands that you treat everyone with respect and compassion. And "everyone" includes yourself.

One day, I told a friend I was disappointed in my wedding pictures. Before my wedding to Tim, I told my friend, I'd been feeling so happy and really good about myself. I'd gained a lot of weight in the preceding months, but I was starting to lose it. Despite the extra weight, I felt beautiful. After I saw how big I looked in the pictures, however, I was devastated and immediately saw myself as huge and unattractive.

This story really offended my friend. It offended her so much that she interrupted me and told me to stop. She said that her impression of me at the wedding was of a beautiful woman who was at home in her "womanness." She said she wasn't going to listen to me talk about myself as "huge."

Why did this story upset her so? Because by the way I was talking, I was dishonoring myself. As soon as she objected to my words, I realized what I was doing. I would never treat another human being the way I was treating myself.

Honor requires that you remember the value of human beings. It demands that you pay attention to feelings, your own and others'. When you hurt people nonchalantly or for your own self-interest, you're not acting honorably.

Being honorable may be hard, but living life without honor is even harder. It's difficult to find real joy in a dishonorable life. So if you want a life filled with joy—a quality life—hold your actions up to the highest standard: the standard of being honorable.

ↄ Becoming Honorable

Day 1: Ask to be honorable.

Day 2: Affirm your desire to become honorable.

Day 3: Act as if you're honorable.

Day 4: Take an honor inventory. What have you stolen? What lies have you told? Whom have you betrayed? Be honest with yourself about what you've done. This may not be fun, but it will be incentive to start acting differently from now on.

Day 5: Think of a time when you acted dishonorably. Did it bring you pleasure? If so, was the pleasure worth the dishonor? Notice the costs of not being honorable.

Day 6: Pretend your life depends on acting with perfect honor. Treat every person, including yourself, with truthful respect today.

Day 7: Do you dishonor yourself? Notice how you treat yourself. Stop yourself from putting yourself down or letting yourself down. Again, do this as if your life depends on it.

Humor (Sense of)

Humor is a hearty belly laugh. It is jokes, riddles and rhymes, puns, teasing, and good times. Humor lives in Giggletown. It is a magic carpet ride that lifts you up from the mundane everyday into the extraordinary everyday. Humor wears mismatched socks and T-shirts with silly sayings. It is always smiling.

MANY PEOPLE HAVE TOLD ME THEY LOVE BEING AROUND me because I boost their ego by laughing at their dumb jokes. I not only have a good sense of humor, but I appreciate good, and even questionable, humor. I'm always looking for laughs, and I often find them in odd places.

One day, for instance, my dog, Muggins, rolled in horse poop while we were on the beach. This isn't a pleasant event. It means I have to bring home an exceedingly smelly dog and give her a bath. I had a busy day of work planned, and giving Muggins a bath wasn't part of the agenda. I could have gotten angry about it, but when I looked at Muggins's delighted expression and her sleek white fur encrusted with clumps of matted horse poop, I laughed. Eau de horse poop is one of Muggins's favorite scents of doggy perfume, and it had been awhile since she'd found some to wear. She was so obviously pleased with herself that I couldn't help but laugh. I wouldn't have been able to laugh if I didn't have a good sense of humor.

If you want to live a quality life, a good sense of humor is a must. You need an ability to find laughter in your day.

In the movie *Mary Poppins,* Mary and the children have tea with Uncle Albert, a jolly man who laughs so much and so heartily that he floats to the ceiling. The children are at first amazed, but then they start laughing too and up they float. Finally, when Mary announces she and the children have to leave, Uncle Albert becomes so unhappy that he begins to sink to the ground. Uncle Albert's sense of humor, his laughter, kept him aloft. When he stopped laughing, even for a short time, he couldn't stay up.

It's not by chance that we call humor and laughter "levity." "We need to add a little levity to the proceedings," people say. Levity also means buoyancy, being light in weight. When people tell you to "lighten up," they're suggesting you find a little humor in a situation. They're suggesting you laugh a little.

Happy people can laugh at themselves. In fact, happy people *must* laugh at themselves. If you want to avoid getting sucked into other people's negativity, you must unhook yourself from bitterness and regret. You must fill yourself with the joy of a sense of humor.

A good sense of humor can elevate your life and fill it with positive experiences. If you're surrounded by the positive energy of humor and laughter, you will attract positive experiences. If you wallow in negativity, you will attract negative experiences.

How do you feel happy, especially when you're not? You

need a kick-start, and a sense of humor is that kick-start. Humor can actually nudge you *into* happiness. A sense of humor will help you smoothly pave the path to a joyful life.

No wonder Uncle Albert floated to the ceiling when he laughed. Laughter transcends the heaviness of life. It raises you up above the mundane, gets you out of your problems and into the joy of the moment—even the moment when your dog rolls in horse poop.

Humorous incidents are all around you. You just need to open your perspective. When a waiter drops lunch in your lap, find the humor in the situation. Believe me, there is some. Humor is always waiting nearby for you to find it. All you have to do is look.

And laugh.

∽ Becoming Humorous

Day 1: Ask to have a sense of humor.

Day 2: Affirm your desire to have a sense of humor.

Day 3: Act as if you have a sense of humor.

Day 4: Read or watch something funny: read the comics, watch a sitcom, or go to a comedy club. Seek out ways to boost your sense of humor.

Day 5: Use your sense of humor in a less obvious place. Find humor in a serious situation. It's there—just look for it.

Day 6: Tell a joke. If you don't know any, ask someone to tell you a joke or look for a joke on the Internet.

Day 7: Right now, laugh. Yes, laugh! You can do it. Just giggle, for no good reason. It may start false, but it will become real as you go along. Notice how much lighter you feel when you laugh.

Independent

Independent is not only capable of standing alone, it enjoys it. Independent needs no strokes from outside sources. It is authentic. It thinks for itself. Independent welcomes new ideas, help, and kind words, but it is no less without them. Independent is majestically one with itself.

WHILE IDLY CHANNEL SURFING ON ONE EXCEEDINGLY LAZY day, I paused on the Home Shopping Network (HSN) to watch Suzanne Somers enthusiastically sing the praises of a pair of earrings from her line of costume jewelry. She and the host of the show were chatting about the quality of Suzanne's jewelry. Suzanne said she doesn't sell anything she herself doesn't love.

Then, however, she admitted she used to try and sell things she didn't believe in. She told a story about her early days with HSN. One day, she said, she was touting the beauty of a piece of her jewelry when she realized she just couldn't do what she was doing. She didn't like the piece, and she couldn't summon up the enthusiasm to convince people to buy it. So, she said, she stopped in the middle of the presentation and announced to the audience that she really didn't like the piece and couldn't in good conscience say she did. The minute she said that, the phone lines, which had been lit up with people ordering the piece of jewelry, went dead.

So what happened? Well, obviously, people thought, *If Suzanne doesn't like it, I certainly don't like it,* which just goes to show how suggestible most of us are.

In "Confident," I talked about how it's possible to be pushed into something you don't want if that something is presented in a tremendously positive light, as the shopping networks are brilliant at doing. My references to these channels might suggest I spend a lot of time watching them. I don't because I find that they suck me into a world where people are discouraged from thinking for themselves.

From time to time, you will be swayed by a powerful argument, and that's okay. The ability to accept another person's viewpoint is part of being open-minded. As much as possible, however, you need to avoid accepting others' opinions without thinking them through yourself.

Being independent means thinking for yourself. It's adopting a set of beliefs that suits you, not your parents, friends, or the rest of society. It's deciding what fashion you like and wearing it, whether it's in vogue or not. When you're independent, you're not going to be easily swayed when someone famous tells you something is pretty, and if you think something is pretty, you aren't going to change your mind if someone famous tells you it isn't. You know what you like, and you act accordingly.

Independence also means doing for yourself. If you want to do something, either for personal pleasure or for financial gain, when you're independent, you know you can do it alone if you have to.

Some people in relationships lack independence. When the individuals in a couple are not independent, the individuals' growth stagnates, which causes the relationship to stagnate. The person you love probably doesn't like all the things you like, and you probably don't like all the things the person you love likes. If you and your partner aren't independent, the two of you may be stuck doing nothing. Sure, you'll be together, but eventually you'll run out of things to talk about. All that togetherness without independent experiences will take all the freshness out of your relationship.

When you're independent, you make your choices based on you, not based on others. You can do this while still being thoughtful and considerate. Being independent means standing alone in your thought and action instead of leaning on others all the time. Of course, sometimes it is important to lean on others for support, but we need to develop the ability to think and act for ourselves so we aren't always dependent on other people's thoughts and actions.

Know your own mind and heart and follow them, not the minds and hearts of others who want to think and feel for you. Be independent.

ᶙ Becoming Independent

Day 1: Ask to be independent.

Day 2: Affirm your desire to become independent.

Day 3: Act as if you're independent.

Day 4: What do you like? Do you know? Or do you follow fads? Today notice your likes and dislikes. Are they yours or someone else's?

Day 5: Think of a time you bought something or did something only because someone talked you into it. How did that feel? Remember the feeling so you can avoid being talked into things in the future.

Day 6: Are you motivated by being popular? If so, ask yourself why. Perhaps you need strokes from others to feel okay. Try giving yourself those strokes.

Day 7: Do something alone today, something you don't normally get to do because others don't like doing it. Go to a museum or the zoo. Go on a long walk. Do whatever it is by and for yourself.

Intentional

Intentional is an arrow aimed right at the bull's-eye. It knows where it's going to land before it ever starts moving. Intentional is fully aware and totally conscious. It is a guide and a teacher. Intentional is the clear single note the orchestra uses to tune up. It sets the tone. It shows the way. Intentional is the starting line and the finish line for every race.

ONE DAY, MY HUSBAND, TIM, SAID TO ME, "THIS EVENING, I'm going to give you a long, full-body massage."

"Great!" I said. I love receiving massages. This was a wonderful gift Tim was going to give me. I was very excited about it, and I looked forward to it all day.

That evening, however, Tim hurt his back, and he couldn't keep his promise. He said, "Will you take a rain check? I'll do it as soon as I'm better."

I was disappointed, but I understood, of course. "Sure," I said.

A week went by. Tim's back healed. A month went by. Another month went by. I never got that massage.

Finally, I said to Tim, "It really hurts me that you didn't keep your promise to give me a massage. I was really excited about it, and I don't understand why you never followed through on what you said you'd do."

Tim said he was sorry. "It wasn't my intention to upset you."

So what *was* his intention?

He simply forgot, you may be saying. He had no intention.

But he did. The act of doing nothing is just as much of an action as the act of doing something. If Tim had the clear intention of bringing me pleasure with a massage, he would have written down a reminder to himself to keep his promise. Instead, Tim had other intentions, perhaps to watch a movie, do work, or whatever. Those intentions created a result he didn't want: me being hurt.

Every action begins with an intention. An intention is a desire or a want, but it's also more than that. It is a use of your will, a sort of inner planning statement that says, "This is what I want from this action or experience."

If every action begins with an intention, then it should be easy to be intentional, right? It would seem to be sort of built into the system. Unfortunately, that isn't completely true. To be intentional, you need to be *aware* of your intentions. You need to be conscious of them. Acting with clear, conscious intention is what being intentional is about.

When you act without being aware of your intention, you may end up with a result you don't like. Action taken on murky or conflicting intentions often creates something other than what you really want.

On the other hand, if you are aware of what result you want from each action, you will always be intentional. For example, if you know you want to experience pleasure when you eat, you will eat whatever you want and enjoy every bite.

You won't care whether the pleasure leads to weight gain. But if you want to be slender, you will eat foods that will facilitate that goal. Your intention to be slender will lead you to bypass the brownies in favor of the broccoli.

But what about when you have conflicting intentions? I have had this problem in the weight area. One of my intentions is to get great pleasure from food. Another intention is to be slender. Another of my intentions is to be healthy. These intentions often are at odds with each other. So what will my actions reflect? My actions will reflect whichever intention is unconsciously more powerful. For me, that means I usually eat more for pleasure and health than for weight loss. This is now a conscious intention on my part, but it used to be unconscious, which generated a lot of frustration for me when I kept getting results I didn't want. I finally had to look at what I was creating and backtrack to what I was intending. When I found the conflicting intentions, I consciously chose one.

Being intentional not only helps you create results you want, it also brings you peace. You won't be blindsided so much when you know what your intentions are. Being aware of intentions requires you to be aware of possible results. Being intentional gives you a chance to avoid mistakes before they happen.

ꙮ Becoming Intentional

Day 1: Ask to be intentional.

Day 2: Affirm your desire to become intentional.

Day 3: Act as if you're intentional.

Day 4: Before you act, as often as possible, ask yourself what your intention is for the action. What do you want from the experience?

Day 5: Before you do things, think them through. What is the likely result of your actions? For example, if you call the man you met at the concert last night, do you think it will lead to the long-term commitment you want or will it lead to a dangerous fling? Following an action to completion in your mind can help you make more intentional choices.

Day 6: If something you do turns out bad today, trace your action back to its intention. What did you want? You'll probably find you had a murky or conflicting intention.

Day 7: If you know you have conflicting intentions about something (for example, part of you wants to stay in a relationship because it's safe and part of you wants out because it's boring), ask yourself which is the more powerful intention. What do you want the most? The answer to this question will guide your actions.

Intuitive

Intuitive is a seer. It is the soul's binoculars. Intuitive is life's instructions whispered in the stillness of the night and in the chaos of busy moments. Intuitive wears subtle clothing. It dresses in pale colors and slips into rooms without fanfare. But Intuitive is the life of the party. When it speaks, everyone needs to listen.

ONE DAY WHILE DRIVING, I HAD THE THOUGHT, *I NEED to get my brakes checked.* This was odd because I'd had no problems with my brakes. Still, in recent months I'd learned that I had a tendency to ignore the intuitive thoughts that popped into my head. I had promised myself I'd start acting on them, and so I had my brakes checked. Turns out they were close to giving out.

From that point on, I started trusting and acting on the little thoughts that popped into my head. Thank heaven I did because one of my little thoughts led to a miracle.

In December 2000, a couple weeks before Christmas, I had a dream about an old boyfriend, Tim. Tim and I went to the same high school, and we dated for a short time when we were both eighteen years old. Tim was a wonderful guy— sweet and considerate, fun and intelligent. We had a great time together. Unfortunately, a tragedy in Tim's life took him away from me. We ended up going our separate ways.

I married, then later divorced. In my mid-thirties, I moved to a small coastal town to start a new life.

Over the years, I thought about Tim from time to time. That December wasn't the first time I'd dreamed about him. He usually showed up in my dreams a couple times a year. This time, though, the dream was followed by a whim, a quiet whisper from my inner voice, *You need to find Tim.*

Well, since my experience with the brakes, I'd been following my intuition, and it had led me to some amazing places. So, of course, I acted on that inner whisper about Tim.

I got on the Internet and began looking for Tim, but having no idea what I was doing, I had little luck in my search. I did, however, stumble onto a Web site called Classmates.com, a database for academic classes. I signed up for my high school class and looked for Tim in the list of names. He wasn't there. Of course not. We had more than seven hundred people in our graduating class. His having found and signed up for the site would have been a long shot.

At that point, I stopped looking and went on about my business. Less than two weeks later, I got an e-mail from Classmates.com informing me that four new people had been added to my class. The e-mail encouraged me to check them out. I went to the site, and lo and behold, there was Tim's name.

My mouth dropped open, and my heart raced. I'd found Tim.

I sent him an e-mail. He answered me. After that, we

began exchanging e-mails on a daily basis. We had virtual conversations in an Internet chat room for hours at a time. After about a week, we spoke on the phone and had a nervous but wonderful spoken conversation. We wrote more. We chatted more. We fell in love. Now we're married.

Lynn A. Robinson, author of *Divine Intuition: Your Guide to Creating a Life You Love,* describes intuition as "a way of knowing, of sensing the truth without explanations."[7] Some people call intuition a hunch or a gut feeling. Some call it a whim or even a flight of fancy. Whatever you call it, however, everyone gets it. But only the intuitive cultivate it and use it.

Becoming intuitive isn't an overnight thing. It takes commitment and practice. First, you need to start encouraging intuition. You stop waiting for whims, hunches, and inner knowing to just pop up—you go looking for them. You do this by consciously asking God or the universe for help with this or that. Ask to be guided and you will begin getting guidance.

Once you get guidance, you must trust it. You can't doubt your inner knowing. You must believe in it.

Then you need to act on the inner knowing you receive. If it tells you to do something directly, like find an old boyfriend, do it. If it gives you information about yourself, someone else, or a situation, use that information to help guide your future actions.

Being intuitive is like having a map and a set of road signs to guide you to the quality life you want. Learn to read the map. Pay attention to the signs. Being intuitive will take you where you want to go.

ᴖ Becoming Intuitive

Day 1: Ask to be intuitive.

Day 2: Affirm your desire to become intuitive.

Day 3: Act as if you're intuitive.

Day 4: Ask for guidance. Ask your inner wisdom or God for help with your decisions and choices as you go through the day.

Day 5: Stay alert for whims and hunches. Listen for those little whispers of wisdom.

Day 6: Pay attention to how often you fail to trust your intuition. Do you get ideas and then argue with them, saying something like, "Yeah, but that won't work because . . ."? Notice how often you doubt your inner knowing.

Day 7: When you get a hunch or a whim today, even if it seems like something silly or unimportant, like a feeling to buy new gardening gloves in the middle of winter, follow it.

Kind

Kind is a sweet smile that wipes away the deepest frowns. Kind will sit with people when they're sick and celebrate with them when they're triumphant. Kind wears a cloak of patience and understanding. It is caring and empathetic. Kind has a touch as gentle as a whisper-soft breeze. Kind sings encouraging songs and murmurs comforting words. Kind is the thread that keeps the fabric of humanity together.

AS I MENTIONED IN "ADAPTABLE" AND "DETERMINED," MY dog, Muggins, has a chronic health problem: inflammatory bowel disease. Most of the time, Muggins does great, but once in a while she feels pretty lousy, and to help her, we give her a thick, chalky medicine. We give her the medicine with a large plastic syringe, squirting it into her mouth and encouraging her to swallow. When I do this myself, it is always a messy process, with much of the medicine ending up on Muggins's chest or the sofa. But when Tim does it, nearly all the medicine goes down Muggins's throat.

Why?

Because Tim is especially kind. Tim, by nature, is an

affectionate, gentle man. When he gives Muggins her medicine, he does so with a soft touch, squeezing only tiny bits
into her mouth at a time and murmuring to her soothingly
as he does so. He strokes her head and tells her how good
she is, and he goes little bit by little bit, not getting at all
upset when she clamps her teeth together and turns her
head away. He tells her he knows it tastes awful, but it will
help her feel better. He keeps stroking and murmuring and
squeezing in more medicine until it's all in, with nary a drop
on Muggins's fur or the sofa.

When I watch Tim do this, I'm chagrined. It's not that I
cram the medicine down Muggins's throat. I think I'm being
gentle. But I've learned that Tim really does have a gentler,
kinder hand than I do.

I'm not sure there's any such thing as being too gentle or
too kind. Sure, you hear people talk of being killed with
kindness, and you hear of children being spoiled with kindness. But do those situations involve true kindness? Often
not. Often what is being offered isn't kindness—it's pity or
guilt.

Just as people often mistake pity for compassion, people
also tend to mix up pity and guilt with kindness. But pity
and guilt come from a place of lack. You feel like the person
is missing something you need to offer them. Kindness, on
the other hand, comes from a place of abundance. It starts
with the love in your heart. Kindness is a true, unselfish desire to treat someone with gentle care.

What's gentle care?

It can be a lot of things. It can be that soft touch that patiently gives medicine. It can be a soothing voice. It can also

be an understanding ear or companionable silence. Some-times it's as simple as a smile.

Being kind comes from the essence of being human. If you watch TV, you might start believing the essence of hu-mans is violence. That behavior, however, doesn't come from the core of people. That behavior is taught. When you were born, you were born kind and gentle. How to be kind and gentle is something you know. It's part of your wiring. If you don't act with kindness, it's not that you can't, it's that you have learned, from your family or society, how not to.

If you've forgotten how to be kind, don't worry. It's easy to remember. Just think about how you want to be treated—how you really *want* to be treated—not how you think you should be treated. More than likely, you want to be treated with care and respect, with a soft hand. If you don't want to be snapped at, you can bet others don't either.

Strip away whatever armor you've built up to deal with the challenges in life and get back to your essence. That's where your ability to be kind is waiting for you.

The more you practice being kind, the easier it will get, because the kinder you are, the kinder others will be to you. It sort of starts growing like a big fragrant flower garden. Kindness is contagious. Catch it and pass it on.

ᴗ Becoming Kind

Day 1: Ask to be kind.

Day 2: Affirm your desire to become kind.

Day 3: Act as if you're kind.

Day 4: If you find yourself wanting to snap at someone today, stop. Take a breath and smile at the person instead.

Day 5: Think about how you prefer people to treat you. Think about the gentle words and touches you like to receive. Now go out there and treat others the way you wish they'd treat you.

Day 6: If you encounter someone in need or someone who's snapping at you, do not judge or ignore them. Spend five minutes being kind. Hug them, sit with them, or just quietly listen.

Day 7: Go out into your day looking for ways to be kind to total strangers. Maybe you can do something as simple as smile at someone who looks upset. Maybe you can listen to a long story or offer a compliment. Hunt for ways to gently connect with people.

Loving

Loving is soft . . . and strong. It moves toward, never away. Loving is a filter that pushes aside the unpleasant and shines a spotlight on the "only." The "only" is that place within each person or animal that receives loving's gift. Loving strokes gently in the empty space of darkest night. Loving sings softly in the noisiest crowds and is always heard.

NOT LONG AFTER MY HUSBAND, TIM, AND I FELL IN LOVE, we were in my SUV, and Tim spilled a soft drink on the seat and carpet. When he did it, he looked at me as if he expected me to yell at him. Even though I wasn't thrilled about the spill, all I said was, "It's okay. It will clean up."

Tim was grateful for my reaction, which was different than what he'd been used to in his life. He thanked me for being so patient and loving.

It's easy to be loving when a romantic relationship is fresh and new. Being patient, as well as sending flowers, giving gifts, and showering your partner with compliments—these things are fun and natural when you're still touched with the dew of a dawning love.

It's also easy to be loving when the person you love is

acting just the way you want them to. When your kids are behaving and your partner is rubbing your feet, when you're boss is giving you a raise and your best friend is telling you how great you are, being loving is like breathing—you do it without thinking about it.

It's easy to be loving when someone is upset or in pain. The instinct to comfort those in distress is also as natural as breathing.

But real loving must be done between the passion of falling in love and the joy of being with people who please you and the satisfaction of helping someone in need. Real loving is done on dark and dirty days when your love is as old and wrinkled as a favorite shirt that's been balled up and stuck at the bottom of the hamper for several months. Real loving is done on the noisy, discordant days when the people you love are being obnoxious, stubborn, or insensitive. Real loving is done when the people around you are full of their own power and are in no way needy or weak.

Unlike loving done when all is well, loving done during confrontation or ugliness doesn't come naturally. It's difficult, and it requires a conscious effort to transcend your desire to walk away from ugliness or lash out in retaliation toward someone who's hurting you with his or her words or actions.

So how can you be loving when you're in these situations? How can you remain loving when you're exhausted after a long day, when you're overwhelmed with work, or when you're not feeling well? How can you stay in a loving place during months and years of being in a relationship with a person, whether a spouse, a child, a parent, or a friend? How? By remembering why this person is in your life in the first place.

It's simply a matter of shining your emotional light on

the good stuff instead of on the bad stuff. Remember why you fell in love with your mate. Remember how you felt about your children when they were first born. Remember what your parents have done for you, the way they read to you and turned on a nightlight to scare away the monsters who lived under your bed. Remember the times when your friends were there for you and all the laughter you've shared. When you put your consciousness on that which you appreciate about people, it's far easier to be loving toward them, even when they're being difficult.

The same, of course, goes for you. Loving yourself is comparatively easy when you triumph, but loving yourself when you're messing up right and left is much more challenging. That's why you need to keep your consciousness on your own true essence. Reach inside and connect with that core that is the divine you, that core that is pure love. When you connect with that part of yourself, it's easier to be loving, even when you've disappointed yourself yet again with your all too human actions.

Being loving is the connecting bond between you and those around you. If you want to be surrounded by love, if you want to fill your life and yourself with love each day, you must be, at all times, loving toward everyone you encounter and most especially toward yourself.

ꙅ Becoming Loving

Day 1: Ask to be loving.

Day 2: Affirm your desire to become loving.

Day 3: Act as if you're loving.

Day 4: List the most important people in your life: your spouse or lover, your children, your parents, your friends. Now write one or two (or as many as you want) reasons why you love each of these people. Keep the list in mind. It will help you be loving, even when someone on your list is being a pill.

Day 5: If someone is upset and attacks you verbally, do not escalate by attacking back with angry words. Do not run away by giving them the silent treatment or by leaving the room. Take a deep breath and go toward the person with gentleness. Tell them you love them or tell them something you appreciate about them. Now you can calmly discuss the problem between you.

Day 6: Tell the important people in your life that you love them.

Day 7: Write down why you like being you. Then look in the mirror and tell yourself *I love you* and mean it.

Nurturing

Nurturing is a warm fire glowing on a winter day, a cup of tea as the sun drops from view, an embrace against the chill of an empty room. Nurturing praises being, but it also lauds accomplishment. Nurturing maneuvers into the sad places and makes happiness possible. Nurturing says, "You are a great person. You deserve happiness," and means it.

A FRIEND OF MINE, DIANNA, IS INVOLVED WITH A PROJECT that tracks peregrine falcons. Dianna and her cohorts look for the birds, bait them with food, trap them, band them for future study, then release them. They later return and catch the falcons again so they can weigh and measure them to chart their growth and health. To the scientist who is at the head of this project, the work is quite straightforward. You catch the birds. You tag them. You let them go. You catch them again. You gather data. For Dianna, this project is far more than that. It's an opportunity to form a bond with majestic creatures.

Dianna's job during the process of banding is to hold the birds. Now, she could *just* hold them. Instead, however, she murmurs to them and strokes them. It's her natural instinct to comfort and care for them. As a result, when the birds are released, they show no signs of being traumatized. She said they usually fly a few feet away, settle on a log, and watch Dianna and her colleagues. Dianna believes, and I agree, that if the birds were upset by the experience, they'd get far away as fast as possible once they're released. Dianna thinks what she does to comfort them helps calm them.

This is nurturing.

Nurturing tends to be a natural response when it comes to children and animals. Most of us have a natural desire to nurture defenseless creatures, be they human, furry, or feathered. But nurturing requires a bit more effort when it comes to yourself and other adults around you.

Do you, for instance, nurture your spouse? Do you nurture your parents, your friends, and your neighbors? Do you, for that matter, nurture yourself?

Possibly no. It's not quite as easy to nurture big, complicated, not-so-cute things like ordinary people. You may not always be in the mood to cuddle your spouse, and you may not want to share gentle touches or kind words with your parents, friends, and neighbors. And if you're like most people, you usually don't have anything good to offer yourself.

If you're going to be nurturing, though, you need to learn how to do it first for yourself, and then for everyone you encounter, not just for your kids when they're being adorable or for your sweet furry pet. Being nurturing is about meeting the universal need for love and encouragement. Nurturing is the stroking that helps you and those you love move forward in life.

Being nurturing is the older sister of being kind. When

you're nurturing, you take simple kindness and deepen it with an intention to soothe, comfort, and encourage.

Nurturing, of course, includes cuddles and gentle touch, but you can offer nurturing in many ways. Nurturing can be a caring word or an upbeat note that says, "Stick with it. I believe in you." It can be a hug, a smile, or a compliment. It can be the sharing of a story about a miracle or about someone beating long odds that will lift up someone who is discouraged. It can be simply listening quietly to someone's pain or celebrating someone's joy. It can be a hug or a smile or a compliment. Nurturing wraps the recipient in love.

Forget coffee. Start your morning with a serving of nurturing and sip from it all day long. Nurturing is a sweet drink of love you can have yourself and offer to others every day. The beauty of being nurturing is that when you nurture others, they tend to nurture you back.

ᴠ Becoming Nurturing

Day 1: Ask to be nurturing.

Day 2: Affirm your desire to become nurturing.

Day 3: Act as if you're nurturing.

Day 4: Practice gentle touch. Use a soft touch to brush the hair from your children's faces, to caress your lover's cheek, or to nuzzle your pet. If you don't have a special person or pet to touch, touch your own face or hair in a gentle caress.

Day 5: Hug three people today. Really hug them.

Day 6: Hug yourself today. Really hug yourself.

Day 7: Focus on encouragement today—encourage yourself first, then others. Encouragement in the form of gentle praise and support is a powerful nurturing force. Replace judgment and criticism with encouragement.

Open-Minded

Open-minded is a puppy—eager and ready. It is bright-eyed and alert, knowing that everything it sees or hears or feels or tastes might be wondrous. Open-minded has no shame. It is proud of what it is and accepting of mistakes. Just as it expects to experience wonder, it expects to be found wondrous. Open-minded believes there is no point in closing the door on seeing or speaking the truth.

MY FATHER AND MY MOTHER DIVORCED WHEN I WAS A SMALL child. I lived with my mother but occasionally visited my father.

On one such visit when I was about twelve years old, my father and I decided we wanted cheesecake, and we went to a bakery to get some. Once there, though, I looked around and didn't see anything that looked the way I thought cheesecake should look. Dejected, I said to my father, "They don't have any."

He said, "Yes, they do," and he pointed to a confection that didn't look a thing like any cheesecake I'd ever seen.

"That's not a cheesecake," I said.

"Wanna bet?" he asked, grinning.

I lost the bet.

The cheesecake I was used to eating was what my mom always made. Her cheesecake, however, is actually more of a cheese pie. But it was what I knew then, and in my pre-teen mind, if it wasn't what I knew, it didn't exist. My father taught me otherwise—and that lesson went way beyond cheesecakes.

My father taught me to look at the world with an eager spirit and an eye for the unexpected. My father's world was an open-minded world.

Open-minded is a quality that creates magic in your life. The magic is the delightful discoveries you make when you live with curiosity—willing to believe new things and see things in a new way.

Imagine for a moment that you live your life inside a single room. It's a lovely room, and you're quite content in it. However, it is limiting because it's a small room. You'd like to go exploring and look at other rooms, but you have a problem. You think the door to your room is locked and you can't leave. So you sit in your room and wonder what it's like in other rooms.

The truth, however, is that the door to your room is not locked. All that is required for you to leave your room is to get up, walk to the door, and turn the knob. This action comes from willingness, a willingness to believe that something beyond your current understanding is possible. Once you take this action, you can open the door to your room. Once the door is open, you're free to explore as far and wide as your courage will allow.

If you refuse to look beyond your past and current experiences, you will never unlock the door to future experiences that are different from what you expect. Unlocking that door by acknowledging that your perceptions are limited and that your world knowledge is even more limited is what will allow you to be open-minded. When you're open-minded, you become a magnet for new experiences, experiences that will help you be a better person and live a happier life.

I, for instance, used to think I was capable of writing only ten or so pages a day when I was working on a novel. That was my limit. I accepted it as the truth. It was just the way it was. One day, though, without realizing what I was doing, I got in the zone during my work time. I wrote more than thirty pages in about four hours time. I was astounded. I had no idea I had that in me. After I did it, I realized I hadn't been open to accomplishing amazing things. Now I regularly write more than thirty pages a day when I'm working on a book, and I allow for the possibility that I can outdo myself anytime I want.

Being open-minded creates possibility in your life. It broadens horizons. It creates, entertains, amuses, educates, and heals. It takes you beyond what you think so you can find what exists outside of the confines of your worldview.

Your thoughts are limiting. Don't let them keep you trapped in a life you don't like. Be open to finding what is outside of the walls you put up with your habitual way of thinking.

If you aren't open to things being different than what you expect, you may miss out on a lot of different cheesecakes. And you may miss out on a lot of life.

☙ Becoming Open-Minded

Day 1: Ask to be open-minded.

Day 2: Affirm your desire to become open-minded.

Day 3: Act as if you're open-minded.

Day 4: List five things you accept as the truth about you. Tell yourself all these things are what have been and you can create something new. Just tell yourself it's possible to create something new and expect it to happen.

Day 5: If you're ill and aren't getting better, resolve that you will do some research to find other possibilities for healing. Look on the Internet or in books. Talk to people. Brainstorm a list of ways you could heal. Become open-minded to new ways of healing. If you're not ill but have some other area of your life than needs work, brainstorm ways of dealing with your problem that you haven't considered before. Become open-minded to new approaches for improving your life.

Day 6: Pick a food you don't like. Buy it and prepare it or order it in a restaurant. Taste it as if you've never tasted it before, with an expectation of liking it. Don't be surprised if you do.

Day 7: If you're dissatisfied with some part of your life, write down how you'd like it to be. Now tell yourself this new reality is possible and begin expecting your life to change. This is turning the knob on the door of that room you've lived in. It will prepare you for acting in ways that will take you into new rooms.

Optimistic

Optimistic expects the best. Optimistic sees rainbows on rainy days. It builds snowmen after blizzards. Optimistic is creative and adaptable. It can feint left, then move right, and it always expects to win the fight. Optimistic sees sunrises even when it's cloudy. It is relentless in its belief in a happy ending.

I USED TO REFUSE TO READ JOHN GRISHAM'S NOVELS. I KNEW he was a best-selling author and his books were supposed to be great suspense thrillers, but I wasn't interested. I actually read three of his books a long time ago, and I wasn't impressed. I just didn't think he was that great of a writer.

Then again . . . it could have been all the green clouding my vision that obscured my judgment.

I was envious of John Grisham. Like myself, he used to be an attorney. He wrote a couple novels that became best sellers, and then he became a multimillionaire. I was saturated green with envy over the man's success. He had what I wanted.

When you're envious, you're acting as if there's a certain amount of success, money, and love in the world. When someone else gets an abundance of it, you think it means there will be less for you. So when you are envious, you limit yourself. You're saying, in effect, *I can't have what they have, and I'm upset about it.*

When you're optimistic, on the other hand, you believe you can get what you want. You know you have the energy to go after it, and you keep yourself positive about your intentions and expectations. You are not defeated by challenges. You don't listen to naysayers. You keep your eyes on the prize, and you keep on walking.

Want to see how that's done? Let me tell you about Evaret.

Evaret is a seventy-eight-year old man with transverse myelitis. He was diagnosed with the disease in 1995, and the doctors told him he would never get out of a wheelchair. The doctors were wrong. They may have known everything they needed to know about transverse myelitis, but they didn't know everything they needed to know about Evaret.

As soon as he was diagnosed with the illness, Evaret began looking for ways to beat it. When he heard about something that sounded promising, he tried it. Soon, he began getting feeling back in places he had been told he'd never have feeling again. Eventually, he was able to stand and even walk.

Evaret's recovery from his illness is an ongoing process. He says, "There's still twenty-four hours in a day; I've got a lot of things I want to do."

Evaret's doctor was so impressed with Evaret's optimism that he asked Evaret to speak at support groups for people with spinal cord injuries. The doctor says Evaret is always cheerful and thankful, even in the midst of a tragic disease.[8]

Evaret is the walking epitome of optimism. Talk about having your eyes on the prize. Evaret knows what he wants, and he's determined to get it. That determination is fed by his optimism. He truly believes he can heal. He expects the best outcome from his efforts. This expectation is what gives him the motivation to work hard every day. All his effort, fueled by his refusal to accept doctors' predictions that he couldn't recover, are the reason he has developed the ability to stand and walk.

That's what optimism will do for you. It will give you the capacity to stand up in your life and walk toward what you want. It will give you the ability to achieve your dreams.

If you don't believe it's possible to get what you want, you won't get it. Optimism is like having the code that will let you break into the secret society of success.

Expect the best, and the best will come to you. When you're optimistic, you embrace the inevitability of getting what you want instead of sinking into the inevitability of failure.

Wouldn't it be better to believe you can have what you want than to be envious of those who already have it? When you're optimistic, you don't waste time on envy. You're too busy creating the quality life you want to live.

↭ BECOMING OPTIMISTIC

Day 1: Ask to be optimistic.

Day 2: Affirm your desire to become optimistic.

Day 3: Act as if you're optimistic.

Day 4: Think of something you want. Several times throughout the day, say "[What you want] is inevitable. I WILL get it."

Day 5: If you feel envy, notice it. It's telling you about something you think you can't have.

Day 6: Once you've realized what you're envious of write "I can have [what you're envious of]" for each item. Then feel what it would be like to have it.

Day 7: As you go through your day today, expect the best in every situation. Catch yourself if you say things like "There will probably be a lot of traffic" or "My proposal will get rejected" or "My boyfriend won't call." Switch every one of these negatives into positives, like "Traffic will be light," "My proposal will be accepted," and "My boyfriend will call."

Passionate

Passionate is an excited child with a favorite toy. It is an avid fisherman waking up at the crack of dawn to try out a new rod. Passionate is enthusiasm dressed up in its best suit. It is a lover, a worker, and a player. It is a focused adult and an eager child. Passionate lives and breathes what it loves. It is the celebration of doing.

MY HUSBAND, TIM, *LOVES* GOLF. HE HAS A PURE, EXUBERANT enthusiasm for the game. He watches it on TV like most men watch football, with avid devotion. He reads about it with focused attention. And the way he talks about it? Well, you should just see him when he gets home from playing a round of golf. He's like a bouncy kid who just left an amusement park, and he wants to tell me about every ride, er, hole.

"I had a great drive on the third hole," he says. "It was straight and long and it landed about six feet from the hole."

"Great," I say with as much enthusiasm as I can (I am *not* passionate about golf).

"Unfortunately, I two-putted," Tim continues, "so I didn't birdie the hole. But I got my par. Then on the fifth hole . . ."

And he's off and running.

Unlike many golfers I've known, Tim doesn't whine and complain about golf. He doesn't go out and have a bad day on the course and then come home and lament how awful it was. He doesn't bemoan his lack of talent or the condition of the greens. He just has a good time with the game. He's alight with optimism when he sees his talents improving even a little bit. Tim breathes in golf the way most people suck in oxygen, only he never takes it for granted. He does it with gratitude and joy.

That's being passionate.

When you're passionate, you care more about just *doing* something than about how well you do it. You don't need what you're doing to make a lot of money or bring you fame and fortune. You're doing whatever you're doing because you love it and because it makes you happy.

The great thing about passion is that often when you are passionate about something, it *will* bring you fame and fortune, and you *will* become great at it. Your attitude, more than your effort, is what makes you successful.

You'd think if being passionate only required that you love something, it would be an easy quality to have. Unfortunately, however, humans have an amazing capacity to block their natural love for things. They do it with barriers such as perfectionism, frustration, and fear.

I, for example, in my heart of hearts, am passionate about writing. But for a long time, I buried my passion under years of frustration and mountains of fear. I hadn't sold a book after years of trying. How could I be passionate about writing? I was afraid I had no writing talent and my dream of being a career novelist would never come true. These negative feelings squashed my passion for writing as effectively as a shoe smashes a spider.

Seeing Tim's passion for golf, however, reminded me how to love something without attaching a bunch of old, ugly garbage to it. Tim doesn't have enough money and time to play as often as he needs to in order to be great at it, but he doesn't let that frustrate him. It's not about being great at it. It's about enjoying it.

You can be passionate about anything. My mother, for instance, for some odd reason, is passionate about pulling weeds. I don't understand that at all, but I enjoy her enthusiasm. Some people are passionate about bugs. This is another mystery to me. But then, I'm passionate about things like dogs' paws. I'm sure that baffles many people too.

Like the quality of sensuality, passion often is tied to sexuality. People understand sexual passion—you know, the hunk-a-hunk of burning love. But many people are not blessed with true passion for the things they do or for their lives in general.

Passion for life is the bottom line of being passionate. If you have enough things in your life you're enthusiastic about, that get you excited and make you feel good, you will be passionate about life.

If you can't think of anything you're passionate about, ask yourself whether you've hidden your passion under negativity. If you still can't figure out what revs your engine, go back in your memories to your childhood. What did you love then? A little excavation of your likes and dislikes can reveal your passions.

What lights you up? Whatever it is, make a place for it in

your life. Give yourself and those around you the gift of enthusiastic zeal. It's a great way to live a quality life.

∽ BECOMING PASSIONATE

Day 1: Ask to be passionate.

Day 2: Affirm your desire to become passionate.

Day 3: Act as if you're passionate.

Day 4: Ask someone what they're passionate about. Then ask them to tell you about it. Notice the way they light up when they talk about their passion.

Day 5: List your passions, the things you truly love to do. If you haven't done one of them lately, ask yourself why.

Day 6: If one of your passions is blocked by fear or frustration, disconnect your need to be good at what you're passionate about from your love of it. Pretend you are good, and the love will bubble up naturally.

Day 7: If you don't have any passions, make a list of what you loved as a child. Ask yourself whether you could be passionate about any of these things now.

Patient

Patient is a dog waiting for its master to come home from work at the end of a long day. Patient is trusting and expectant. It is hopeful and faithful. Patient knows that what it wants will come in time, and it is willing to wait. Patient knows that everything that needs to happen is happening, even in the stillness of what looks like nothing.

HANGING FROM THE ROOF OVER THE COVERED PART OF MY back deck is a set of wind chimes. In the winter, with the nearly constant wind on the coast, I get used to hearing the wind chimes on my deck daily. So when the soothing rich sound stopped one day, I noticed the silence. Looking outside, I quickly saw the source of the problem. My chimes had become entangled. Wrapped up together, they could no longer move freely and make that peaceful sound I love so much. All they could offer was a dull clunk.

When I saw the chimes were tangled, I was too busy to do anything about it. Every day for a couple weeks, I wanted to go out and untangle the chimes, and every day something came up to distract me. In the end, I never had to do anything.

One day, after a particularly brisk windstorm, I heard a sound I hadn't heard in a while. I heard my chimes. I looked outside, and there they were, hanging straight and untangled.

When something tangles up in your life, when a relationship becomes awkward, a job becomes difficult, or some conflict arises, your natural instinct probably is to rush in and fix the problem. But often, efforts to untangle a problem results in more tangles. Sometimes the "fixing" makes things worse.

Time is often your best friend. Problems that seem unsolvable have a way of solving themselves when you relax, take a step back, and patiently wait to see what unfolds. Life has a way of bringing in winds that, by their own power, shift things around, often for the better. In other words, some things have a life, or timing, of their own.

So how do you know when you need to take action versus when you need to do nothing?

Trust your gut. If you're not sure exactly what to do, do nothing until you get an idea. Doing the wrong thing is worse than doing nothing at all. Similarly, if you keep getting pulled away from the problem by other, more pressing situations, trust the timing. Sometimes you really are better off when you just let things happen.

Doing nothing is an important part of being patient, but it isn't *always* the right thing. Usually you do need to take action. Even then, while you're moving toward your goal, you need to be patient.

For years I have submitted my writing—fiction and nonfiction books, essays, and so on—to publishers, editors, and agents. The submission process is one that requires almost superhuman patience. The review time is always long, and when my work is rejected, I have to try again . . . and again. It goes on and on.

Many times during the last several years, I've given up on sending out my writing. Eventually, though, I'd gather my strength and submit again. The ability to keep going even when your goal eludes you is another important part of being patient. When you're patient, you can wait calmly and expectantly for what you want to reach you or for you to reach it.

You can always spot patient people in a long line. They're the ones standing quietly still. They're smiling and looking around, chatting calmly with someone nearby, or reading. They're not tapping their feet, fidgeting, looking at their watch, or complaining. You can learn from patient people. Practice stillness. Practice being okay with a lack of movement in your life.

Whether you do nothing or something, you need to pave the way to your destination with a thick layer of patience. Being patient will give you a solid road to stand on while you hang in there until whatever you want shows up on the horizon.

∽ BECOMING PATIENT

Day 1: Ask to be patient.

Day 2: Affirm your desire to become patient.

Day 3: Act as if you're patient.

Day 4: Think of a time in your life when you finally got something for which you'd had to wait a long time. Remember how good it felt? Keep that feeling in mind as you wait for what you want now.

Day 5: Do you have a problem that needs untangling? Ask yourself whether you need to just let it be. Try letting it be at least for today. Expect it to resolve over time, and tell yourself you can wait.

Day 6: Do you have a goal you've been working toward for years, a goal you've started giving up on? Today get in action again. Take a small step toward the goal. Tell yourself you can keep going and you can wait for success.

Day 7: Look at the clock several times today. Notice how it keeps moving and how it takes you out of places you don't want to be. Want to be done with a project or a class or a chore? Notice how the passage of time gets you what you want. Remind yourself that you don't need it all right now. Time is your friend.

Persistent

Persistent wears comfortable hiking boots because it knows it has to go to the end of the trail. It doesn't get stopped by blisters, aching muscles, bad weather, or other people. Persistent might sit down to rest a bit, but it never gives up.

IN THE EARLY NINETIES, I BEGAN GETTING IDEAS FOR SHORT essays. The ideas came to me as easily as mosquitoes in the spring, and unlike mosquitoes, I didn't swat them away. I started writing essays. At first, I didn't know what, if anything, I was going to do with them. But then it occurred to me that my little essays might make good newspaper columns. I decided to see whether I could write for a newspaper.

I bought a book on how to become a columnist. The book, however, wasn't exactly encouraging. It cited the overwhelming odds of breaking into the journalistic world as a columnist. It said that often new columnists have to write for no payment in order to break in. Just as often, columnists can only find room for their work in small weekly papers. The book suggested that if you're willing to take on the challenges of being a columnist, you should write a few samples and then approach an editor.

Undaunted by the overwhelming odds against success, I decided to give it a try. As the books advised, I wrote seven sample columns and a proposal letter and sent them to the editor of the local daily paper.

Beginning with a daily paper was beyond a long shot. The books said that few columnists break into daily papers right off the bat. But I figured, why not make the attempt? As the books suggested, I hand-delivered the samples and letter to the paper's editor. He said he'd read them when he had a chance. When after three weeks I hadn't heard from him, I called him and left a polite message asking whether he'd had a chance to read them. He called back and said he hadn't but he would. Three weeks later, I left another message. He called back and said, "Persistence such as yours pays off. I promise I will read them."

A week later, he sent me an e-mail that said he'd read the columns. He liked them a lot but had some concerns about whether I could keep up the quality over time. I called him and asked him whether I could send him fourteen more samples to show I could keep up the quality. He said that was fine. So I sat down and wrote fourteen more samples.

After I sent those off, I waited again. And left follow-up messages. And waited. And called again. Finally, the editor e-mailed me once more. His e-mail began "You are very talented. Let's have lunch."

We had lunch, and he took me on as a paid columnist. That was almost five years ago. I've been writing a weekly column ever since.

The whole submission process from when I left the first samples to when we had lunch took six months. Some of my friends thought I should give up and move on to another, smaller paper. I figured I should keep going until I had the answer I wanted. Like the editor said, persistence pays off.

Being persistent is the ability to keep going even when the going is tough. Like its cousins—determined and patient— persistence knows how to move past obstacles. When you're persistent, you stay focused on the goal. You do whatever is necessary to get there.

Inventor Charles F. Kettering knew about persistence. He applied for more than three hundred patents in his lifetime, and his industrial research laboratory produced new all-electric starting, ignition, and lighting systems for automobiles in the early 1900s. Kettering once said, "Keep on going and the chances are you will stumble on something perhaps when you least expect it. I have never heard of anyone stumbling on something sitting down."

If you know where you're going, even if it's just a vague knowing, like the desire for joy, love, or inner peace, getting there requires that you keep moving, even when you have no idea what to do next. When I say "keep moving," I don't necessarily mean take action. Sometimes, as I talk about in "Patient" and as I had to do when I was working to get my column in the newspaper, you need to wait. This waiting, though, is purposeful waiting. It's waiting with an expectation of knowing what to do next. It is not giving up. Like Kettering said, if you're sitting down, as in not trying at all or giving up, you are guaranteed failure. If you keep trying, you may still fail from time to time, but at least you have a chance to succeed.

Whatever you're trying to accomplish in your life, you

must keep going. Your goals are worthwhile. They deserve committed, unwavering action. They require put-one-foot-in-front-of-the-other sort of dogged movement. They require persistence.

∽ Becoming Persistent

Day 1: Ask to be persistent.

Day 2: Affirm your desire to become persistent.

Day 3: Act as if you're persistent.

Day 4: As with "Patient," think of a time in your life when you were persistent and it paid off. (This might be the same time you were patient. Patience and persistence often work hand in hand.) Remember how good it felt to reach your goal. Remind yourself that you know how to be persistent.

Day 5: Think of something in your life now that you need to be persistent about. Write it down in big letters on colorful paper. Put the paper up someplace in your home where you can see it. It will remind you to keep on going, even when the going gets tough.

Day 6: Sit down. Now try and cross the room from this position. It's not possible, is it? Remember this exercise when you think about giving up on something.

Day 7: Think of a time when, while you were in action toward a goal, you stumbled over a new idea or had a great experience. Remind yourself of the great things that can happen when you're persistent.

Playful

Playful wears a striped beanie hat with a whirling pinwheel on top. Playful likes to sneak up and pounce, then laugh in delight. It takes great joy in things like stuffed animals, games, jokes, bubbles, water balloons, trolls, and coloring. Playful is ageless. It has no inhibitions. It is spontaneous and sure. It lives in a magical world of joy.

WHEN I DECIDED TO START EDUCATING MYSELF ABOUT FI-nances and the stock market, I explored several books and Web sites, all of which I had to force myself to read. Although I like money, managing money bores the patooties out of me.

So it was with great joy that I discovered the investment information source that engaged me enough to keep me reading even through my substantial resistance. I found the perfect place for me when I found www.fool.com, and I found the perfect investing book when I found *The Motley Fool Investment Guide* by David Gardner and Tom Gardner.[9] The information at the site and in the book was solid and easily accessible, but it was more the attitude behind the information that I liked. That attitude was one of playfulness. Heck, what would you expect from authors who had their picture taken wearing jester hats? I mean, these guys, even though they deal in the serious world of high finance, know how to be playful. I can relate to that.

Harpo Marx once said, "If all else fails, stand on your head." When the world seems to stop making sense, the only thing to do is to look at the world with a totally different perspective. What better way to do that than to stand on your head? But if you can't physically stand on your head, being playful is just as effective.

Being playful is throwing out the rules and finding a way to have fun. Being playful happens outside the normal boundaries of everyday life. It's throwing a Frisbee on windy days and laughing delightedly when the disk comes right back at you and wallops you in the belly. It's dancing while you do housework and finding it inordinately funny when you trip over the vacuum cleaner while boogying to hope-lessly outdated disco music. It's making love with all the lights on and discovering new positions that even the writ-ers of the *Kama Sutra* didn't think of. Never mind that the position in no way could lead to any sort of climax. It's the trying that's the fun. It's the play that heightens the inti-macy, and it's the intimacy that later leads to that climax.

Not just sexual climax. Playfulness takes you to the cli-max of life, the high points where you disappear into a haze of laughter and fun. You can get to this place, as I do, by playing with your dog or your spouse. You can get to it by playing with your kids (or someone else's kids, for that mat-ter). You can get to it by throwing things, juggling things, reading things. You can get to it by dancing, by laughing, by singing. You can get to it on the ground or in the air. You can get to it alone, with someone you love, or with a total stranger. Whenever you play, you have unlocked the door to ultimate joy.

Play is the foundation for the rest of your life. You simply cannot build a successful career, relationship, or personal life without play. Serious foundations are too brittle. They crack under pressure. They have no give for when the ground moves under you.

And believe me, at some point in your life, the ground will move under you. Everything you know will be turned upside down. Your ability to be playful will get you through those times. Playfulness is like a "get out of jail free" card. You can stockpile these cards by incorporating play into your daily life, by making play as important, maybe even more important, than anything else you do.

To help you access your ability to be playful, call on the qualities of childlike and fun-loving. Use your sense of humor. These qualities will lead you to being playful, and being playful will help you develop these other qualities too.

Really, I'm not playing around here. You need to be playful if you want to live a great life.

ᔢ Becoming Playful

Day 1: Ask to be playful.

Day 2: Affirm your desire to become playful.

Day 3: Act as if you're playful.

Day 4: All right, here it is again. You did it with "Childlike" and "Fun-Loving," but don't let that stop you. Buy another toy. You can never have too many toys.

Day 5: Call up a friend or invite your spouse to play today. Do something fun like toss a ball around or go see a funny movie.

Day 6: On your way to someplace today, play a car game like "I spy something [fill in a color]." Or look for funny vanity plates. Or sing silly songs. Make your travel time playful.

Day 7: Using the guidelines in "Fun-Loving," find a child or a pet to play with. Spend at least ten minutes in silly play.

Present

Present is a spotlight on what is. It's single-minded and totally attuned to the task at hand. Present lives only in one moment, not concerned about the next one. Present is clear. It does not get distracted. It is never in two places at once. It never tries to be something other than what it needs to be. Present is the perimeter around every action, the frame within which every picture is displayed.

I USED TO USE MY DAILY TIME WALKING ON THE BEACH TO work through problems. I'd hash over situations I needed to handle and have imaginary conversations with people I needed to communicate with. If I was angry or upset about something in my life, I could churn up an entire hour of beach-walking time without ever noticing the frothy ocean waves next to me or the beautiful blue sky above me. If I was really worked up, I could even manage to get all the way home from the beach (a five-minute drive) without seeing much of anything. Somehow, I made it home safely anyway.

What did I miss along the way? A lot of things. One day, though, I missed something very important.

On that day, in the evening, I talked on the phone with my friend Dianna.

"How are you doing?" she asked.

"Not good," I said.

"I figured as much," Dianna said.

"Why's that?"

"Because I saw you on the road this morning, and I waved. You were looking right at my car, but you didn't see me."

I felt awful. Dianna's car isn't a standout on its own, just a beige Toyota sedan. But she has vanity plates that are very distinctive, and she usually has her even more distinctive yellow lab, Jake, riding with her, with his beautiful head out the window. How had I missed her? "I didn't see you," I said unnecessarily. "I would have waved if I had."

"I know," Dianna said. "It's okay. So what's going on?"

And my understanding friend and I moved on to what had been upsetting me that day.

Thankfully, Dianna didn't take offense at my negligent snub. I, however, never forgot it. It showed me that I wasn't being present in my life. That disturbed me.

The incident with Dianna, however, wasn't the first time I'd noticed how much I miss by getting caught up in my thoughts.

For example, getting a massage is one of my very favorite ways to spend time. Why is it, then, that I sometimes spend the entire massage puzzling over some problem or planning some future event when I could be relishing the pleasure of having someone knead my aching muscles? Because, again, I'm not being present.

Being present means being acutely aware of what's going on at that moment in time, not just peripherally aware. Being present is being highly attuned to what is happening right now. It's being focused on what's in front of you at any given moment.

To find the pleasure in simple activities, you must be present. Zen philosophy advises that you focus on whatever it is you're doing because you can get enjoyment from almost any task. There's joy to be found even in washing dishes, in the tactile sensations of the water and the soap.

Being present assures that you will get every ounce of experience from your experiences. It guarantees that you will get the most out of every minute you're alive.

This is a good thing, you may be thinking, when it comes to pleasurable activities. But what about painful experiences?

Being present is essential for the unpleasant in life as much as it is for the pleasant. Resistance, both physical and mental, tightens you up and exacerbates whatever discomfort you're in. When you're present to pain, you can relax into it. When you relax into it, you ultimately feel less pain because you let go of your resistance. Being present to pain, both physical and mental, helps you get through it faster. It also helps you learn from it.

When I suffer from depression, for instance, if I try to cover up the pain with compulsive eating, I get even more depressed and I stay depressed longer. However, when I stay present to the despair and the darkness within me, when I acknowledge and feel it, it passes more quickly. I also am more able to see the lessons in the experience.

When you're present to life, you will discover that your days are filled with more wonder and more miracles than you could ever have asked for. You'll find it all in one single moment, the one that you're living right now.

∽ BECOMING PRESENT

Day 1: Ask to be present.

Day 2: Affirm your desire to become present.

Day 3: Act as if you're present.

Day 4: Right now. Stop. Where is your mind? On what you're doing or on what you did yesterday or what you're going to do next? Notice the difference in how it feels to be thinking about what is done or what is to come and how it feels to just be thinking of what you're doing now.

Day 5: Several times today, stop and notice whether you're totally present to what you're doing. Are you focused on what you're doing or is your mind wandering?

Day 6: If you're in some kind of pain, try not to mask it. Feel it. Go into it and acknowledge it. Ask it what it has to teach you about yourself. Then be ready to let it go.

Day 7: Think of times when your mind habitually wanders. Maybe you're cooking or working or driving. Maybe you're even making love. Think about what you miss when your mind isn't on what you're doing.

Purposeful

Purposeful has a secret, a special, bright secret. As it walks through each day, purposeful is moving toward that secret. Purposeful has a filter that can sift out extraneous noise or activity. It hears only encouraging words, calming music, and the shout of success. Purposeful knows why it's here. It rises each day with confidence in its place in the world.

YOU OFTEN HEAR CHILDREN, AND EVEN ADULTS, SAY, "BUT I didn't do it on purpose." The words are offered up as an excuse for some action that isn't welcomed by someone else. When little Sally tears little Billy's favorite shirt while they're playing, she may say when Billy gets angry, "But I didn't do it on purpose." This doesn't make Billy feel any better. The end result is the end result.

I know I don't feel any better when someone says in chagrin, after letting me down in some way, "But I didn't do it on purpose, you know." Let's say a friend promised to do something for me, like pick up a book I need while she's in the city, and she assured me she wouldn't forget. I counted on her to get the book and took no action to get it myself. When my friend returns and I ask about the book, she tells me that she forgot and that she feels bad but didn't do it on purpose.

My friend's excuse doesn't change what she did or didn't do. The end result, her failure to get the book, is the same, whether she did it on purpose or not.

Now, what if my friend had been purposeful to start with? What if she had decided on a result (following through on what she said she'd do—pick up the book) and then aimed her actions accordingly (such as write a note to remind herself or stop at the bookstore first)? Then she'd have reached a different end result.

This is being purposeful. Being purposeful, you'll notice, is similar to being intentional. The two qualities are not exactly alike, however. You need them both if you want to have your actions lead to results you like. Think of intentional as the seed, the idea behind your aim toward what you want. Purposeful is the aim and throw itself.

When you take action in your life, you need to do so with focus. Your intention in taking action must have some clear reason behind it. Even if it's spontaneous, action has purpose, such as to have fun or relax. Every situation in your life has something to teach you. If you're living purposefully, you will be living with the aim of comprehending the lessons you encounter.

To be purposeful, you need to figure out what matters most to you. For example, using the example of my friend's situation, if she starts her day knowing that she promised to pick up the book I needed, this promise becomes an essential part of her day. It is essential not because I want the book but because she's made the promise and because keeping promises is something she wants to do. That is part of her purpose for that day. So as she goes through her day, although she may get distracted by music she hears or a conversation she has, she will remember her purpose: to keep the promise she made at the beginning of the day.

In order to live purposefully, you need to review your actions each day. Have you done what you said you'd do? Have you finished your projects? Have you stayed true to your aim and kept on toward your goals? Being purposeful requires that you be aware of what you're doing. Checking in with what you've done helps accomplish this.

All purposeful action is important. It keeps you on track. It prevents accidents, and it helps you be the kind of person others can count on. But the most important purposeful action you can take is to live your entire life on purpose—to live in concert with your soul's reason for being on the planet.

The best purposeful action is that which supports your soul's purpose. When you act with a higher aim in mind, you're generally acting from some inner truth, your soul's truth. And when you act from your soul's truth, you find contentment and happiness unlike any other (see also "Centered").

Practice living purposefully. Be aware of what you're doing. Have an end in mind, a result you can be proud of. Let purposeful living lead you to your soul.

꒲ BECOMING PURPOSEFUL

Day 1: Ask to be purposeful.

Day 2: Affirm your desire to become purposeful.

Day 3: Act as if you're purposeful.

Day 4: Make sure your actions have focus. Pay attention to what you need to learn in all situations you're in.

Day 5: As you look at what you need to do today, figure out the most important things. Plan your day accordingly.

Day 6: If you find yourself sidetracked by something, ask whether that something serves a purpose. Does it help you meet a goal or priority? If not, does it help you develop an inner quality like being playful or childlike? If so, great. If not, move on to something you've decided is a priority. These priorities have purpose behind them.

Day 7: At the end of the day, review what you've done. Did you stay on track with your aims? If so, reward yourself with some special treat. If not, think about how you could have made different choices to remain purposeful.

Resilient

Resilient bounces like a big rubber ball. You can throw it down, but it comes right back up. Resilient may get wet, but it dries right off. It may get dirty, but it shakes itself and is clean again. Resilient wears a suit of armor that deflects defeat. Setbacks might dent the metal, but the armor remains strong. It is both flexible and strong—and ultimately indestructible.

DURING THE LAST SEVERAL YEARS, LIFE EVENTS HAVE knocked me down many times. First, my marriage to my first husband failed. I went from living in a large, expensive house being supported by a husband who made a comfortable six-figure income to suddenly needing to find a place to live. I also had to accept that my income was now going to be less than a sixth of what it had been.

Having your life flattened in that way isn't much fun, but I didn't stay down. I popped right back up. I bought a modest house, and I set up a careful, small budget. I began focusing on creating a life that suited me perfectly.

Part of that life was establishing an independent, more comfortable source of income. To that end, I decided to participate in a multilevel marketing business. I was sure it would give me the income I wanted. It didn't. In fact, I lost a significant amount of money in the endeavor.

Splat. I was down again. But I put the loss behind me and bounced back, intent on creating the income I needed with my writing. That process alone knocked me down several more times. The attempt to publish novels. Splat. The attempt to become a copywriter. Splat. The attempt to syndicate my weekly column. Splat. Each time I hit the ground, I stayed there for a bit while I watched the little birdies fly around my battered head. Then I got back up and moved on to another project.

I've been knocked down by depression and physical health challenges. I've been knocked down by failed relationships. Even since I became healthier and happily married to my soul mate, I've been challenged. My father died. I dealt with the grief and began handling his estate, and I bounced back. Then my mother and my stepfather began having health problems. I coped with stress that comes with having ill family members, and I bounced back.

While all of that was going on, my beloved dog, Muggins, was quite ill. The saga of her health problems alone has knocked me down multiple times. Splat, splat, splat. Each time, I gather myself and come up with some new course of action to help her.

That's what being resilient is about. Resilience is the support system of persistence. If you're not resilient, you won't be able to be persistent, because every time you fall down, you'll stay down. You can't keep moving through your life when you're down. You can't walk through your life if you're not on your feet. I don't mean that literally. You can roll through life in a wheelchair or you can participate in life from your bed. Being on your feet doesn't require that you stand up physically. It does, however, demand that you bounce back mentally, emotionally, and spiritually. You must not let your spirit and your psyche lay prone for long if you want to have a fulfilling life.

Jean-Dominique Bauby knew this. In 1995, Bauby was the editor in chief of French *Elle* magazine. He was the father of two. He had an active life. But then he had a stroke, one that left him in a coma for twenty days. When he woke up, he was flat on his back and stuck in a body that no longer worked. Only his left eye functioned. He used that eye not only to see but also to communicate.

By blinking to select letters one by one, as a special alphabet was slowly recited to him over and over, Bauby formed words, sentences, and thoughts. He also eventually formed a book, *The Diving Bell and the Butterfly,* an amazing achievement of intellect and spirit.[10] Even though he was trapped inside a body that couldn't move, a sensation that he likened to living inside a diving bell, his mind was free to fly like a butterfly.

Bauby was the epitome of resilience. His illness eventually claimed his life, but he never gave up until he left this earth. He bounced back, even while living with the most horrible of misfortunes.

If you want to be resilient, aspire to be like Bauby. Do not let your disappointments and failures keep you down. Pop back up after every loss, every trauma, and every struggle.

You never know when fortune and success are going to come your way. You won't see them coming if you're flat on your proverbial back.

ꙮ BECOMING RESILIENT

Day 1: Ask to be resilient.

Day 2: Affirm your desire to become resilient.

Day 3: Act as if you're resilient.

Day 4: Go out and buy a rubber ball. It will remind you to be resilient.

Day 5: If you encounter a failure today, say, "I bounce back like a rubber ball," and get right back on track with what you need to do.

Day 6: Think of the times life has knocked you down and how it felt to triumph after you got back up. Really feel it. That's what being resilient feels like. Keep this feeling in mind as you go through your day.

Day 7: Fall down. That's right. Now. Fall to the floor. Now get up. See how easy that was? Remember this whenever life knocks your spirit down.

Responsible

Responsible is a shepherd overseeing the flock. It looks out for others while it looks out for itself. It plays, but it always finishes its work too. It laughs, but it knows when to be serious. It spends money, but it knows when to save. Responsible has perfect balance. It can manage obligation while living a life of freedom. Responsible knows where the buck stops.

WHEN I CLERKED FOR AN APPELLATE COURT JUDGE, I SAW all kinds of cases, a lot of them negligence cases. In these cases, the plaintiff was alleging that someone else caused his or her injuries or loss. Of course, sometimes this is true. If a guy is driving down the road obeying all traffic laws and otherwise minding his own business when a drunk driver runs a red light and plows into his car, there's no question that the drunk driver is responsible. Many lawsuits, however, aren't so clear-cut.

For instance, consider the young man who ignored prominent no-trespassing signs that warned a construction area was dangerous and said, in no uncertain terms, to KEEP OUT. When the man decided to ignore the signs and jog in the area, he fell and became a quadriplegic. Was this

his own fault? He didn't think so. He thought the construction company should have done a better job of keeping him out by putting up more effective barriers.

Believe me, when you see enough cases like this, you start taking a look at whether you try and pass blame for things you did that didn't work out too well. You learn to stop whining and start saying to yourself, *Yeah, I did that. Oops. Now I will deal with it.*

That's what responsibility is all about. Dealing with it. You need to deal with the day-to-day mundane aspects of life and you need to deal with the consequences of your choices.

Responsibility has two parts. First, you handle your affairs with integrity and timeliness. This means paying your bills on time, paying your taxes, and being honest about both. It means repaying loans you borrow. It means spending only what you can pay for, not racking up a lot of debt just so you can have the latest fashion footwear. It means keeping your home in good order so your neighbors don't have to look at something trashy. It means being law-abiding. It means providing care to the beings—children, elderly people, or animals—in your charge. I could go on, but it boils down to this: Handling your affairs with integrity and timeliness requires meeting your obligations, to yourself and to others, when those obligations are due.

The first part of being responsible is essentially common sense and maturity. It's about keeping your life in order, whatever that takes.

The second part of responsibility is actually less work, but often, it's a lot more difficult to do. The second part of being responsible is accepting that *you* are the reason you make the choices you do. This requires that you give up excuses. You no longer get to point fingers at other people or places and say, "He [or she or it or the devil] made me do it." You're the boss. You're the one in charge of you. You made you do it. Not your old boyfriend, not your best friend, not your parents, not or your kids, not the drug dealers, not the tobacco, fast food, or alcohol companies. You.

When you're responsible, you know you make your own choices. Sure, the world puts temptations and opportunities in your path, but you decide what to do with them. If something you choose ends up bad, you are the reason it did and you are the one who needs to figure out how to deal with the consequences.

When I asked my husband, Tim, what being responsible meant to him, he said, without hesitation, "Seeing things through to the end."

"What do you mean exactly?" I asked.

"Well, you know, being responsible is, well, being responsible."

Uh, yes. That helps a lot.

But I know what he means. Whether it's meeting your obligations in your personal or business life or accepting the consequences of your actions, responsibility is seeing things through to the end. Being responsible is just being responsible. You know how to do it, so see it through to the end.

ᴗ Becoming Responsible

Day 1: Ask to be responsible.

Day 2: Affirm your desire to become responsible.

Day 3: Act as if you're responsible.

Day 4: Take a responsibility inventory. Divide your life into the areas of your business, financial, and personal affairs. List some of the things you need to do in these areas. Do you do them? Grade yourself on how well you meet your obligations. If you get a low grade by ignoring your obligations in some areas, resolve to do better.

Day 5: When you make a mistake, resist the temptation to blame it on someone else. If you don't like the consequences of one of your choices, don't get angry. Just say, "Oops, yeah, I did that." If you need to apologize to someone, do so.

Day 6: If there is some obligation you've been avoiding, such as paying something or taking some action, do it today.

Day 7: If you have people or pets in your care, make sure you do the best you can for them today. Be sure you see them as a priority in your life every day.

Romantic

Romantic is a single rose on a special day. It's candlelight and soft music. It's surprises and sensual delights. Romantic is love in action. It is thoughtful love, creative love. Romantic is love in a tuxedo or a long gown. It is the titillation that keeps marriages alive for the long haul. It is the reason people want to fall in love.

TIM AND I WERE MARRIED ON MAY 7, AND NOW, ON THE seventh of every month, Tim brings me red roses. The first year we were married, he brought me one rose. The second year, it was two. We're up to three now. The roses are simple, wrapped in plastic and tied with a bow. They have no ferns or baby's breath dressing them up. They're just roses. Just an affirmation that Tim loves me and celebrates the day we were married. Just romantic.

Romance is the frills and finery of love. Being romantic is telling your spouse you love him or her, even when he or she knows you do. It's offering to give him or her a foot rub using scented oil. It's reading poetry aloud and holding hands in the grocery store.

Romantic people buy their lovers gifts for no particular reason, but they also remember anniversaries. Romantic people kiss and touch often. They dance, they make love, and they curl up together to watch romantic movies.

Despite what many people think, romance doesn't require much money. Romantic people find ways to express their love even when their resources are limited. If a romantic person can't afford diamonds, he or she buys beads. If a romantic person can't afford a fine restaurant, he or she serves pizza by candlelight.

Being romantic requires some creativity. When you combine that creativity with a desire to share your heart, you will bring pleasure to the person you love. For example, Tim and I picked out and bought our wedding rings and my engagement ring. Since we already had the rings, I knew Tim was going to propose. Because he wanted the timing of the proposal to be a surprise, however, I didn't know when it would happen. Still, I wanted to contribute my own bit of romance to the event. So I bought a brass key chain with "YES!!!" engraved on it. I carried that thing around in my purse or pocket for several weeks, just waiting for Tim to propose.

He finally did, in a beautiful spot in Port Townsend, Washington. We were on a day trip and had been hiking around Fort Worden State Park, the old military fort where *An Officer and a Gentleman* was filmed. On top of one of the bunkers, Tim pulled the ring from his pocket and asked me whether I'd do him the honor of allowing him to be my husband. I said, "Wait."

Then I dug around in my backpack while Tim looked on in bemusement. Finally, I pulled out the key chain and handed it to him. When he read the inscription, he laughed. "That's perfect," he said. And we kissed.

That was romantic.

When you're romantic, you will have closer and richer love relationships. Of course, romance alone won't keep a relationship vibrant. Good relationships require many, if not most, of the qualities in this book. But it's tough to have a truly wonderful relationship without some romance.

Romance is more than just the garnish on good love. It's the spice. Imagine chili without chili powder or cinnamon rolls without cinnamon. If you want the real thing, the whole thing, you need the spice. When you're romantic, you have the spice to put in your relationships.

Remember, however, that you don't have to be in a love relationship to be romantic. You can be romantic on your own just as well. Eat by candlelight. Wear silky loungewear. Sip wine under the stars. Buy yourself flowers and special treats. Nibble chocolates in a bubble bath. This is romance too because it's an active expression of love—for yourself. Expressing love for yourself boosts your self-esteem and enjoyment of your life. Also, when you can love yourself in a romantic way, you'll be better at loving another in a romantic way.

Being romantic puts the spice in love. The spice in love is what brings love to life. And living a life filled with love? What could be more romantic than that?

ꝇ Becoming Romantic

Day 1: Ask to be romantic.

Day 2: Affirm your desire to become romantic.

Day 3: Act as if you're romantic.

Day 4: Eat by candlelight tonight.

Day 5: Buy flowers for someone you love today (that can be you).

Day 6: If you're in a relationship, buy your partner a surprise gift today. If you're not in a relationship, buy yourself a gift.

Day 7: Make a list of fun ways you can be romantic. Brainstorm. Include things like tucking a love poem in your spouse's wallet before he or she leaves for work or treating yourself to a long bubble bath in a dimly lit room while you listen to music you love.

Self-Aware

Self-aware is a well-examined flower. Self-aware knows its own heart. It sees every flat surface and every crease of what it is. It is not afraid of its own darkness. It celebrates its light. It hears its own voice, and it knows its scent. Self-aware embraces all aspects of what it is. Self-aware is its own best friend. Self-aware is love.

IT WAS A SULTRY SUMMER EVENING. A SLIGHT BREEZE FROM the west filled the air with the ocean's scent. My dog, Muggins, thrashed around near the wild honeysuckle at the edge of the woods surrounding my house. Crickets sang. An occasional crow flew overhead and let loose with a raucous "Cawwwww."

I lit a candle and set it on the simple white, round, plastic table on my deck. I was dressed in a floor-length satin caftan with blue, gold, and red swirls. Not traditional wedding garb. But then, this wasn't a traditional wedding. On this quiet summer night in the stillness of twilight, I was getting ready to marry myself.

No, I'm not a narcissist. Nor am I a spinster who can't find a mate. In fact, I'm now happily married.

I was at the time, though, a thirty-seven-year-old woman

who had divorced following a thirteen-year marriage and who was just learning how to be alone. Until a couple years before, I had been so busy being what people thought I should be that I hadn't had the time to learn to be who I am. This quiet ceremony I was about to begin and the vows I was about to recite were a symbolic representation of my intention not to repeat an old pattern. It was a celebration of my resolve to be self-aware.

Being self-aware means knowing yourself. This is not as easy as it sounds. Some people think they know themselves because they know their favorite foods, favorite color, and whether they like their job. But self-knowledge goes much deeper than this superficial stuff. To be self-aware, you need to know not only what you like and don't like but also what you feel and what you believe.

Sometimes self-knowledge is ugly, and because of this, many people want to avoid being self-aware. I don't like, for example, that I tend to hoard money and am often judgmental. This is not an awareness that makes me happy. I also don't like knowing I carry around a lot of anger that bubbles up when I'm under stress. This is pain I don't want to feel. Yet I know if I avoid the ugly knowledge and the pain, I'm abandoning myself, and I took a vow when I married myself not to do that.

Closing down parts of yourself will never get you a quality life. Living for others without being cognizant of who you are will not take you where you want to go. If you don't know where you want to go because you're so busy keeping track of where other people want you to be, you will never get where you're meant to be. You will spend your life blind to the magic you came here to create.

Carl Jung said, "Your vision will become clear only when you can look into your own heart. Who looks outside, dreams; who looks inside, awakens." When you're self-aware, you look inside regularly. You will not sleepwalk through your life dreaming the dreams of the frustrated. You will not docilely follow someone else along a path that's totally wrong for you and ultimately end up at a destination that brings you no joy at all.

When you're self-aware, you know your own soul. You know your passions and pains. You become committed, first and foremost, to you, and that commitment allows you to make commitments to others that make your life and theirs the richer for the connection.

To become self-aware, you must stop looking outside yourself for information about you. Never let others tell you what you're worth. Don't let others tell you how you feel or how you think. Don't let them tell you what you like or what you should be doing. In fact, when you hear the word *should,* alarm bells need to go off within you. These warn you that now is a good time to ask yourself what you *want* to do to create your best life.

Begin making friends with yourself. Pay attention to what makes you feel happy and what makes you feel sad. Notice what you want and don't want. Learn how your mind works. Ferret out your weaknesses and your strengths and accept them both. Make yourself the most interesting person you ever get to know.

When you become self-aware, you do more than say "I do" to yourself. You say "I do" to a rich, quality life.

∽ BECOMING SELF-AWARE

Day 1: Ask to be self-aware.

Day 2: Affirm your desire to become self-aware.

Day 3: Act as if you're self-aware.

Day 4: Resolve to get to know your feelings. Begin listing what makes you happy and what makes you feel bad.

Day 5: Get to know what you want and what you don't want. List both.

Day 6: List your strengths. Be proud of them. List your weaknesses. Accept them.

Day 7: Resolve to marry yourself. Create a simple ceremony and write some vows promising to know and love yourself, honor and respect yourself, forgive yourself, care for yourself, and use your inner resources to create a quality life for yourself. Drink a sparkling cider toast to your commitment to you. If you want, buy yourself a ring to symbolize your self-union. If you don't want to marry yourself, perhaps have a simple ceremony to commit to being self-aware. Light a candle. Promise to get to know yourself. Celebrate the wonder of you.

Sensual

Sensual is a pig basking in cool, wet mud on a hot, sweltering day. Sensual can take something simple, even messy, and find pleasure in it. Sensual celebrates all senses—taste, smell, sight, hearing, and touch. Sensual relishes tactile sensations. It appreciates subtle scents and new flavors. It rejoices in the tiniest sounds and the most everyday sights. Sensual experiences the world fully and celebrates it.

MY DOG, MUGGINS, IS A SENSORY DELIGHT. I LOVE STROKing her silky fur and nuzzling her warm body with my nose. I love inhaling the happy scent of her, that great smell of canine after play. I love smelling her feet too. Yes, I said her feet. Have you ever smelled a dog's paws, the pads of their feet? They smell like corn chips. Really. It is a most satisfying scent, a both grounded and active scent.

I love listening to Muggins too. When she sleeps, she often emits soft rumbling snores and little sucking sounds as she twitches her feet. I delight in the even, graceful gliding, whooshing sound of her breath as her ribs rise and fall. When she's awake, I enjoy her play growls, her excited whines and yips, and her happy "arrwoos."

Of course, I like watching Muggins too. I enjoy staring at her sweet, whiskered muzzle. I like the crisp lines of her markings, and I often trace the outlines of her black patches where they mingle with her white fur. I love her little tail with its white tuft of hair that flutters when she wags it. I could stare for hours at . . . okay, I could go on, but you get the idea. My enjoyment of Muggins depends on my using as many of my senses as I can. It hinges on my being sensual.

When you hear the word *sensual,* I'm betting you rarely think of things like dogs' paws. People often associate the word *sensual* with erotic or sexual situations. When you hear "sensual," you probably think of a gorgeous man or woman, not a furry dog with corn chip–scented feet.

But if that's what you think you need to be sensual, you're limiting yourself. Sensual does not mean sexual. It means being devoted to your senses. It is an ability to garner pleasure from every sensory experience. It's an attitude of reverence for your capacity to see, smell, taste, hear, and touch all the wondrous delights of life.

In any given day, you are provided with literally hundreds of opportunities to be sensual. You see trees and flowers and people and buildings. You smell leather and wood smoke and lemons and perfume. You taste rich coffee and sweet donuts and tart apples and tangy salads. You hear laughter and birds and music and rustling leaves. You touch soft pillows and warm skin and slick plastic and smooth ceramic. If you're aware of every one of these chances to indulge your senses, you will enrich your life tenfold.

Being sensual means being vibrantly alive. When you immerse yourself in your world with all your senses, you will get the most from every experience you have. You will appreciate every place you go, every person you see, everything you eat.

Sensuality is an active form of gratitude. It's also access to experiencing great pleasure in life.

Things you might initially think of as something you don't want to sense can bring you pleasure as well. For instance, my husband, Tim, used to apologize to me when he got sweaty after working out or playing golf. "Oh, no, don't kiss me," he'd say. "I smell sweaty."

I would lean into him, put my nose to his warm skin, and inhale the scent of him. Yes, it was sweaty, but it was *him.* Instead of turning me off, it turned me on. Tim doesn't apologize for being sweaty anymore.

Speaking of turn-ons, even though sensuality isn't the same thing as sexuality, I will talk about sexuality for a moment. Sexuality is an ability to enjoy and celebrate the sexual aspect of yourself. One of the reasons many people aren't sexual is that they cannot let themselves go enough to enjoy their body and that of their partner with abandon. Many people are too concerned about how they look or how they're performing or what their partner is thinking to let themselves fully integrate with the bliss that loving sex between two committed partners can create. One way to step out of the confines of judgment and into the exquisite delight of pleasure is to let go of what's going on in your head and pay more attention to what's going on with your senses. Being sensual will help you be more sexual.

Being sensual will help you be more, period. It will help you be more present, more grateful, more free, more attentive, more playful, more loving . . . the list goes on. Most important, being sensual will help you be more joyful.

∾ BECOMING SENSUAL

Day 1: Ask to be sensual.

Day 2: Affirm your desire to become sensual.

Day 3: Act as if you're sensual.

Day 4: Savor your food. Really taste what you're eating.

Day 5: Linger over something beautiful. Just stop and stare at it: a lovely child, a cute animal, a gorgeous sunset or tree. Drink in the beauty.

Day 6: Touch a lot of things. Really feel them. Notice textures and temperatures. What do you like? Do you like warm and smooth? Cool and coarse? Find more things like that to touch.

Day 7: Buy yourself something with a great scent, such as a candle, perfume, or a sweet confection. Also, listen to music at least once today. Really enjoy the scents and sounds you encounter.

Spirited

Spirited is a wild child, eager to do, to be, and to go places. It puts its face up to the sun and grins broadly, appreciating the warmth. Spirited marvels at everything, from a simple oak leaf to a majestic redwood. Spirited has a twinkle in its eye and a bounce in its step. It is ready for action, full of energy and purpose. Spirited charges after its dreams and rejoices in life.

MY HUSBAND, TIM, IS THE DIRECTOR OF A SMALL COMMU-nity choir. The choir practices on Monday evenings, and Tim comes home from these practices sometime after nine o'clock. Although he's home plenty early to get to bed at a reasonable hour, Tim often stays up quite late on Monday nights. This is because he's so spun up after choir practices that he has trouble getting to sleep.

Tim, you see, loves directing this choir. He loves music in general, but the choir is, as they say, a labor of love. Tim has a vision for this choir. He has taken on a small group of singers, most of whom can't read music, and he dreams of creating a vibrant, blended sound that will uplift and in-spire every audience that hears them perform.

To that end, Tim spends a lot of time picking the music

the choir will sing and even more time guiding his choir to sing it the best they possibly can. When he sees the choir making progress, it fills him with such satisfaction that it's as if the satisfaction is a string tugging him upward, and were it not for gravity, he'd bounce right through the roof. Tim is full of eager energy and purposeful drive for his choir. The stamina and drive come from being spirited about the choir.

Webster's Ninth New Collegiate Dictionary defines spirited as "full of energy, animation, or courage." In other words, being spirited is being so excited about what you're doing that you bubble forth with energy and enthusiasm. When you're spirited, you're driven to go after dreams, not from a place of duty or obligation but from an inner force that propels you in the direction you want to go.

This doesn't mean, however, that being spirited is reserved only for when you're pursuing some "important" goal like putting together a choir or going after a desired job or relationship. You can be spirited in everyday tasks as well.

Tim, for example, is spirited about far more than his choir. When he mows the lawn, for instance, he sets out to create the best-mowed lawn he can create. He mows the lawn a bit differently every time, creating new patterns in the grass. When he's done, he'll say something like "I did triangles today. What do you think?" He comes up with purposeful energy even for something as "unimportant" as mowing the lawn.

This kind of eager drive to do well and have fun while doing it is contagious. It's enjoyable to be around. All spirited people are enjoyable to be around. Spirited people are like warm sunshine on a cold day. You just want to be in their presence. These people are going places, and you want to go with them. You're drawn to them. They give off a glow of happiness. They buzz with energy.

But you don't have to get that kind of energy vicariously. You can create it yourself. Whenever you approach any activity, ask yourself why you're doing it. Think about what you want to create with your actions. When you know where you want to be in life, you can easily tap into the energy you need to get there. That energy is within each of us.

Being spirited takes being passionate to the next level. It adds energy and drive to a love of doing something. Being spirited means being enthusiastic. When you're enthusiastic, you have zeal for what you're doing. You're excited about your activities. If you can't summon up this feeling for anything you do, you might ask yourself why you do the things you do. It's possible that much of what you're doing is not what you want to be doing and is therefore not leading you to the life you want to lead. If that's the case, now is a good time to think about making different choices. Choose to be involved in activities—jobs, relationships, and hobbies—that you can be excited about.

It's also possible that you're doing what you want to be doing but that you've squelched your spirit under fear, anxiety, or some other kind of pressure. Remember how fear can kill passion? It kills spirit too. For example, if Tim were afraid he'd fail to create the choir he envisions, he wouldn't be spirited about it. But instead of putting his attention on such thoughts, he fills his mind with the expectation that he will succeed. That expectation creates his enthusiasm.

Your life is like a song ready to be sung. You can sing it

flat, creating a listless sound, or you can sing it with energy, creating the beautiful sound of spirited music.

ᴄ Becoming Spirited

Day 1: Ask to be spirited.

Day 2: Affirm your desire to become spirited.

Day 3: Act as if you're spirited.

Day 4: If something you're doing feels tedious, ask yourself why you're doing it. If the reason is important to you, remind yourself of the reason and let that reason create enthusiasm for what you're doing. For example, sometimes I feel that doing research for books is tedious, but when I remind myself of the book I'm planning to write, I feel my enthusiasm returning, and I immediately become spirited again.

Day 5: Whenever your energy slacks off, get out a piece of paper and write down what it is you're working to create in your life. For example, if you're feeling tired in the afternoon while you're taking care of your kids, write down what kind of lives you envision for your grown children. Focusing on what you're moving toward can renew your energy.

Day 6: Take a fear/anxiety inventory. List your fears and anxieties. Look to see whether any of them are blocking you from being spirited. If so, draw a line through the fear/

anxiety, and write what you want to create instead. For instance, my list would include "I'm afraid my book won't be good enough." This fear is blocking me from being spirited about writing. So I draw a line through the fear and replace it with "I want to write a magnificent book."

Day 7: Put some bop in your walk today. Walk with spring in your step. This simple action can create energy in your body that, in turn, can create spirit for whatever you're doing.

Spiritual

Spiritual is a magnificent throne that sparkles in a ray of sunshine. The throne is a throne of truth, purpose, and direction. Spiritual is connected to everything, and everything is connected to it. It is divine. It comes from the divine, and all it touches is divine. Spiritual is a gentle breeze that stirs up from within. It caresses and comforts, guides and directs.

I KNEW JAN FOR A COUPLE YEARS BEFORE WE BECAME GOOD friends. I was happy when our friendship grew stronger and we spent more time together because I had been drawn to Jan since I'd first met her. There was something about her, something peaceful and real, that made me want to get to know her. She had a kind of calmness about her that drew me in. I didn't know where that calmness came from, but I wanted to be near it.

It wasn't until I began spending a lot of time with Jan that I realized what it was she had that I didn't at the time. Jan is spiritual. She radiates the truth of her spirit. She's connected with her soul. She's aware of the sacred in life, and she searches for and relishes the divine.

Jan is a seeker of truth. She wants to know herself in

order to understand her place in the world. She wants to see the divinity within herself and not get bogged down in only the physicality of her life. When she finds herself obsessing over some mundane aspect of life, like her weight or whether something looks good or not, she takes a breath and reminds herself that what matters is that which cannot be seen: the spirit.

She wants to know others as much as she wants to know herself. In knowing others, she can understand her connectedness with them and with every part of the universe. She wants to see the divinity within others and not get bogged down in only the physicality of those around her. When she finds herself judging others on the basis of something they have done or how they look, she takes a breath and reminds herself that what matters is that which she cannot see: the spirit.

Jan is spiritual.

I am too. Now.

It took me several years to get here, and though I don't believe I exude the kind of calm and peace that Jan does, I am, as much as she, a seeker of truth. My goal each day is to live in concert with my soul. I look for inspiration because it leads me to the flow of my days. It takes me to divine possibility. It connects me with the most real part of myself, and when I'm connected with that part of myself, I can then connect to that part of everyone else.

Spirituality is the basis of understanding, connection, and peace. It gives you a context for the rest of your life. It gives you a solid base from which to become what you were meant to become. When you are spiritual, you will be aware of opportunities you are meant to seize and guidance you are meant to follow. When you are spiritual, you have a better chance of staying on your soul's path, your true path, the one that is perfect for you.

The paths of spirituality are as varied as the souls seeking them. If you look for spirituality in the world, you will see it in dozens of religions, mountains of dogma, and piles of books. It will take form in the mainstream and in the bizarre. All of it and none of it is valid. In other words, all of it can help lead you to your spirit; but none of it, in and of itself, will make you spiritual. Being spiritual is something you live and breathe, from within. It cannot be done for you, and it cannot be found outside of you.

If you want to be spiritual, you must start with getting to know yourself. Know your dreams and fears, your loves and hates. Now, add to that knowledge a daily practice that connects you to a Higher Power. This practice can be meditation, prayer, or reading spiritual texts. It can also be spending time in nature, feeling the connectedness between you and the divine. But you must do something to create a flow of energy between you and a Higher Power. To be spiritual, you need to ask questions and seek answers in places you've never looked before. You need to believe in the divine and the sacred and search for both every single day.

The divine is in every aspect of your life. It's in your relationships with others and yourself. It's in your thoughts and feelings. It's in your surroundings. It's in your goals and actions. When you're spiritual, you celebrate the perfect order of the universe by pulling that perfect order into your own life. A spiritual life is one of balance, one of quality. When you're spiritual, you honor your mind, your body, your heart, and your soul by living as purely and truthfully as you can.

Many of the other qualities in this book can spring from being spiritual. When you're spiritual, you're more centered and therefore have wondrous flow in your days. You're more intuitive and therefore experience more synchronicity that can guide you in all you do. You're wiser because you're connected to guidance that leads you to truth. Live a spiritual life, and you will be amazed at the magic that results.

∽ Becoming Spiritual

Day 1: Ask to be spiritual.

Day 2: Affirm your desire to become spiritual.

Day 3: Act as if you're spiritual.

Day 4: Say a prayer—to God, to Buddha, to angels, or to whatever Higher Power makes sense to you. Say a prayer asking to connect to your soul and the souls of others.

Day 5: Read a book on spirituality, whatever kind of book appeals to you. Although a religious practice isn't necessary to being spiritual, you can use the beliefs and behaviors of religions to enhance your spirituality. So if you're moved to read a book on a specific religion, go for it. Otherwise, find a book on spiritual thought. Go to the spirituality section of your bookstore or library and start browsing. Pick out a book that feels right to you (maybe it will fall from the shelf) and begin reading.

Day 6: Meditate. Quiet your mind, and for just five minutes or so, sit and pay attention to the rhythm of your breath. When your mind wanders, gently call it back. A quiet mind can access your Higher Power.

Day 7: If you're in a religion that doesn't make sense to you spiritually, ask yourself what you need to make it meaningful.

Strong

Strong can lift up the world. It squares its shoulders and takes on any burdens it must take on. Strong can handle anything, even when it thinks it can't. Strong measures success by survival. Sometimes that means forward motion. Sometimes that means just enduring. Strong is quietly triumphant.

IN THE EARLY NINETIES, MY EX-HUSBAND AND I HELPED MY parents move all their belongings, belongings that included a heavy piano, a number of large appliances and awkward pieces of furniture, and dozens of boxes of books, into a new home. My ex and I did much of the heavy lifting.

At one point in the move, as I was manhandling a large piece of furniture onto the truck, I noticed my dad watching me with an odd expression on his face.

"What?" I asked.

"You know," he said, "you're a lot stronger than you look."

"I lift weights," I said, and I felt gratified that getting up early all those mornings to work out was paying off. I have to say, though, that except for a few times in my life, the actual physical strength weightlifting gives me isn't something I use often. Sure, lifting weights makes my back stronger. It helps keep my bones in better condition, and it burns calories. However, the biggest payoff I get for lifting weights is that it makes me feel strong.

I'm not talking about physical strength. I'm talking about mental, spiritual, and emotional strength. I'm talking about having inner strength.

Inner strength is the strength of discipline and tenacity. It's the strength of growing. It's the strength of independence. It's the strength to hang on to goals. It's also the strength, when necessary, to let go.

The resolve to make changes in your life must come from within. It arises from an inner knowing that you can do the hard thing. Knowing assures you that you have the courage to plunge off cliffs into the unknown. Being strong is what allows you to be courageous.

Weightlifting has helped me develop this kind of knowing because I hate weightlifting. I really do. It's not fun. It's hard. But I do it anyway. I do it because it's good for me. Knowing that I have the strength to make myself do something difficult helps me do hard things in other areas of my life.

Of course, often I forget I have such strength. I've been in bad relationships and taken far too long to leave because I was afraid of being alone. Once I did get up the strength to leave, though, I was happier, every time.

Sometimes I'm afraid to start things, projects like new books I want to write or some business idea I'd like to pursue. I'm afraid the work will be difficult, and I'm also afraid I'll fail. Then I remember that I'm strong. I delve within and connect with my inner strength, and it leads me into the new challenge I want to take on.

Sometimes I'm reluctant to continue with something that has become tedious or difficult. I consider giving up. I want to set my burden aside and plunk my butt down on the edge of the proverbial road of life. I'm tired—mentally, emotionally, and spiritually, not to mention physically. Then I remember that I'm strong. My inner strength gives me what I need to get back on the road. Being strong helps you be persistent too.

Inner strength is like a personal generator. Often, when you're trying to start, continue on, or leave a part of your life, you have help available to you. There's nothing at all wrong with that. Asking for help and getting it can require strength as well. But if what you need to do can't be done by others, you will have to find a way to do it yourself.

When you have the personal generator of strength, you don't need to plug into the electrical outlet of other people or resources. All you have to do is turn on your own juice, and you have what it takes to do whatever you need to do.

ഴ Becoming Strong

Day 1: Ask to be strong.

Day 2: Affirm your desire to become strong.

Day 3: Act as if you're strong.

Day 4: If you don't already lift weights, give it a try. If weight-lifting doesn't appeal to you, begin some other physical regimen that builds physical strength. The discipline and effort this requires will not only help you build inner strength but also put you in a strong state of mind.

Day 5: Ask yourself whether there is something in your life you need to let go. If so, write down your intention of doing so. Facing the need to let go can be your access to finding the strength to doing the actual letting go. Strength often comes from accepting necessity.

Day 6: Ask yourself whether there is some difficult step you need to take toward something, like going to the doctor about a lump or applying for a job. Write down your intention to do this. Again, facing up to a problem can give you the strength you need to deal with it.

Day 7: Say "I am strong" several times today. Write down these words and tuck the paper into your wallet. Look at it often.

Thoughtful

Thoughtful is aware of others. It opens doors for people, remembers birthdays, and brings hot lemonade to friends suffering with a cold. Thoughtful knows just what to give and when to give it. It knows just what to say and when to say it. Thoughtful is a butterfly with bright wings of support that lands on the shoulders of others. Thoughtful reaches out, beyond itself, to wrap the world in caring.

WHILE MY HUSBAND, TIM, AND I WERE TALKING ON THE phone one day before we were married and before he moved in with me, he was folding towels.

"You know," he said, "you're going to have to show me how you like your towels folded."

"What?" I asked, not sure I'd heard him correctly.

"Your towels," he said. "You might like them folded a certain way, and it doesn't matter to me. We'll do it the way it suits you."

I was speechless. I didn't even know a man existed who would fold towels in the first place much less care about folding them in a way that suited me.

Talk about thoughtful.

But then, that's Tim. He's one of the most thoughtful men

I've ever known. He does things like put toothpaste on my toothbrush when he's doing his own. He turns on the electric blanket on my side of the bed to warm it up for me before we go to sleep. If he has to get up early, he'll set out his clothes the night before so he can grab them quickly and quietly in the dark. If he uses up all the toilet paper, he gets out a new roll.

Tim's thoughtfulness isn't limited to me. At the grocery store, he pulls carts out for people who walk up to the cart line at the same time he does. If someone is having a problem lifting something, Tim offers to help. If they can't reach something, he does it for them. Tim is always looking out for others.

Being thoughtful means being aware of other people and trying to do things that might be helpful or comforting to them. Being thoughtful asks that you step out of the box of your own concerns and include those of others. You think about what other people need—you are *full* of *thoughts* about others.

Being thoughtful is a sort of precognition. What would someone else like? What do they need? You ask those questions, and you come up with an answer. Then you do what you think would be liked or needed.

You may be thinking all this sounds sort of like being a servant. Or a slave. Guessing and then meeting peoples' needs seems a bit obsequious. They have names for it when it's done in the workplace or in school—it's called, unpleasantly, brown-nosing, or more pleasantly, buttering up. When it's done to the extreme, to the point of losing one's self, it's called codependency.

On the surface, fawning over someone or enabling them

may seem the same as being thoughtful, but these actions are quite different. They're different because when you're being thoughtful, you're not motivated by getting something. When you're being thoughtful, you aren't trying to get approval or a paycheck or get someone to like you or give you a raise or good grades. Being thoughtful is about basic, unselfish caring. Thoughtful comes from the heart. It's voluntary. You do what you do not because people want it or need it but because it makes you feel good.

When you're thoughtful, you expect nothing in return for what you do. Although thoughtfulness may grow from the seed of an unselfish desire, it grows exponentially. Whatever thoughtfulness you put out, you tend to get back in spades. Of course, that's not why you're thoughtful. But it's a great perk for just being, well, nice.

ᔕ Becoming Thoughtful

Day 1: Ask to be thoughtful.

Day 2: Affirm your desire to become thoughtful.

Day 3: Act as if you're thoughtful.

Day 4: Hold doors open for as many people as you can today.

Day 5: Think of something a loved one needs and do it for him or her today.

Day 6: Be alert to what a stranger may need. Help him or her if you can.

Day 7: Make a list of things you'd like people to do for you: bring you coffee, let you pull in front of them in traffic, help you with your coat, and so on. This list will help you be more aware of what you can do for others.

Trusting

*Trusting is a fragile flower blooming unprotected in an open field.
It lifts its head to the sun and rain and doesn't worry about the occasional passing feet. Trusting has an open heart. It assumes the
best. It takes big bites without sniffing or tasting a little bit first.
Trusting believes what it hears and accepts what it sees.*

As I related in "adventurous," my husband, Tim, moved
in with me following a month of long-distance communication. I had known Tim before that month, but it had been
twenty years before, and so when we first reconnected, I
asked him a lot of questions about the kind of person he had
become.

"Do you have any vices?" I asked him at one point. "Smok-
ing, drinking, drugs, cheating, or lying?"

"Nope," he answered. "But I am addicted to the TV
show *ER.*

I assured him *ER* wasn't a vice. I liked the show too.

I asked him about how he liked to keep a house. Was he
a slob?

"Nope," he said again. He told me he did the cleaning during his marriage, and he liked to keep things neat.

I asked question after question, and he gave me answers. Mostly the answers came via e-mail.

E-mail is not the most discerning form of communication. When you speak with someone face-to-face, you can read them if you're paying attention to body language. Even over the phone, you can get an idea of truthfulness from tone of voice, hesitation, and other such cues. But when someone types information, it comes across pretty flat. No nuances to discern.

So for all I knew, Tim was lying through his teeth when he answered all my questions. He could have told me he was the prince of all princes, and I wouldn't have known otherwise.

Tim often gave me wonderful compliments via e-mail too. One day, for instance, in response to me telling him the beach had been beautiful when I'd walked on it that morning, he wrote, "Of course it was beautiful. You were on it."

When I related this to my dad, he said, "I don't think this guy is real. Real men don't talk like that. I think he's a figment of your computer."

And so he could have been. But I preferred to think he was for real. I trusted what he said was true, and because of it, I agreed to have him move across the country to be with me.

For the record, everything he said *was* true, and he does say things like that beautiful comment all the time. It's the truth of who he is. I'm so glad I trusted him.

Trusting in its truest form means expecting things to be okay. To trust life is to hope that life will bring you what you need. You go out into the world expecting that the experiences you have will be for your highest good. You believe that your hardships will teach you, your efforts will fulfill you, and your triumphs will sustain you. Trusting life is reliance on the wisdom and peace of the universe.

Trusting life isn't easy. What about the disasters life brings your way? How can you trust that all is good if, for example, you lose your spouse or your child to tragedy or you face catastrophic illness? The way you do it is you remember that life as you know it is only one small part of what life is. Your spirit is far more than the limitations you encounter in your physical form. Being trusting of life is remembering what you truly are.

You can become more trusting of life as a whole if you remember the little ways you're trusting every day without thinking about it. For instance, when you drive, you trust that other drivers will stay in their lanes. When you plant grass and flowers, you trust that they'll grow. When you go to bed at night, you trust you'll wake up in the morning.

While you're trusting life, you also need to trust others. To trust another is to hope that they will bring you what you expect from them. When you're trusting, you believe people will say what they mean, do what they say they'll do, and be who they present themselves to be.

Trusting others isn't easy either. What about the liars and the people who don't keep promises? There's a fine line between trusting and being foolish. If you are too trusting of people, you can be taken advantage of. Yes, you'll encounter people who aren't who they say they are. But if you turn away from trust and *expect* to encounter these people, you will miss the vast majority of people who can be trusted. You will be attuned to letdown, not to fulfilling good expectations. If you expect to encounter trustworthy people while at the same time keeping your intuitive antennae extended for any signs of falseness, you'll have mostly positive trust experiences.

If you think trusting life and others is difficult, those challenges are nothing compared to trusting yourself. Trusting yourself means that you believe in you. You believe you can do what you want or what you feel you're being called to do. You can make positive choices. Trusting you means being true to you.

Failure to be trusting has a tendency to create messes in your life. When you struggle and resist life, people, and yourself, you're going to stumble a lot. If you want to walk surely and smoothly through life, you need to learn to be trusting. That's the way to make good decisions.

It's true. Trust me.

❧ BECOMING TRUSTING

Day 1: Ask to be trusting.

Day 2: Affirm your desire to become trusting.

Day 3: Act as if you're trusting.

Day 4: Tell yourself you expect life to bring you what you need for your highest good.

Day 5: Interact with people in a trusting way. Expect them to keep their word and to be real with you. Notice that with this attitude, you encounter more honest people.

Day 6: Ask yourself today whether you trust yourself. Do you doubt your decisions? If so, look back over your mistakes and see whether you might have ignored your inner wisdom (intuition) when you made the mistakes. Resolve to trust your intuition.

Day 7: Ask yourself what you might miss by not trusting. Is, for example, the man whose invitation to dinner you turned down because you didn't trust his motives your soul mate? Maybe he isn't, but maybe he is. Be aware of your gut in-stincts. If your gut tells you to trust and you ignore your instincts because you've been taught people aren't trust-worthy, you may be missing a lot of miracles in your life.

Truthful

Truthful is a clear note sung high and strong in a song of otherwise garbled melody. Truthful is not an exhibitionist—it doesn't have to show itself to the world, but it's comfortable doing so. It has no problem standing naked in a spotlight. Truthful has nothing to hide. Truthful speaks when it has to, and when it does, its words are a current of air that lifts away the heavy weight of secrets and false words.

I USED TO HAVE A FRIEND WHO ALWAYS SAID EXACTLY WHAT he was thinking whenever he thought it. He had no problem telling people they were fat. He delighted in informing people when they made stupid mistakes. Essentially, what this man did was share his judgmental thoughts.

Although being truthful is a quality you need to develop, saying exactly what you're thinking is not. Being truthful doesn't require that you share every judgment and observation you may have. There's a difference between being truthful and being careless with your mouth. Also, a judgment is just a judgment—not necessarily the truth. Judgment and truth are often oranges and apples.

When you're truthful, you choose to share only information that is honest and real. You may not volunteer to your friend that you hate her new boyfriend, and even if she asks you what you think, you won't blurt, "He's a jerk. He's a loser, and he's ugly to boot." But you will tell her you don't have a good feeling about the man. You might tell her you don't get good vibes from him or he's not the person you would choose. When you're truthful, you may put a pretty coat of tact on your honesty, but you don't smear your real opinions with the mud of fantasy or fiction.

In many areas of life, being truthful isn't too difficult. It's just a matter of avoiding lies. When you're thinking one thing, you don't say another. When you want something, you don't pretend you want something else. This part of being truthful only requires that you be willing to face the possible disapproval or confrontation that could occur when people disagree with you or don't like what you want.

There is, however, a more complicated aspect of being truthful. To be truthful, you have to peel away the illusions that blind you to truth. In other words, when you're truthful, you can't go around kidding yourself. Being truthful starts with being truthful to yourself, and being truthful to yourself starts with knowing yourself (see "Self-Aware").

Several years ago, I got involved with a man I'll call Fred. After two weeks of being with Fred, I knew the relationship would never work. He was confrontational, selfish, frequently inconsiderate, and had several other qualities I didn't enjoy. At the time, though, I was lonely and in need of affirmation from the opposite sex that I was attractive and desirable. So I ignored the truth in my heart that said it was wrong for me to be with this man, and I pretended we had a future. I wasn't blatantly lying to him or to me—I kept trying to convince myself a future with the man was a possibility. In other words, I kept trying to change the truth. But I knew, deep down, I was wasting my time and his time with the relationship.

What was the cost of my failure to be truthful? Well, I lost a year during which I could have been focusing on other more positive things in my life. Also, my dog suffered because the man and I fought often, and the fighting upset Muggins tremendously. My health suffered as well—the confrontation took its toll on my immune system, and it triggered a lot of eating binges.

When you're not truthful, some part of your life will suffer. You may hurt your health, as I did. You may hurt people or animals you care about. You may squander your resources (time, energy, and even money) and miss opportunities for something better in your life.

Being truthful is hard work. It requires constant vigilance. You can't be lazy with your thoughts or your mouth if you want to be truthful. You need to be aware of what you're feeling and thinking to mine the truth from your psyche. Then you need to be diligent about the way you communicate so you will share the truth you've mined.

Even though it's difficult, the payoff for being truthful is worth the effort. Mining the truth is better than mining gold or diamonds because the truth brings you riches more valuable than any precious metal or gem—the riches of a great life.

∽ Becoming Truthful

Day 1: Ask to be truthful.

Day 2: Affirm your desire to become truthful.

Day 3: Act as if you're truthful.

Day 4: Pay attention to what you say. Tell only the truth or say nothing at all. Make sure you keep your word. Make your promises truthful by doing what you say you'll do.

Day 5: Ask yourself whether you're being honest with yourself—in all areas of your life. Are you trying to convince yourself of something you know isn't true (like you're in the right relationship or job)? Look in the mirror and tell yourself what you believe to be the truth. See whether it looks and feels right.

Day 6: If you have a judgment or criticism you're tempted to share today, ask whether you really need to do so. Does it further a relationship or a goal? If so, okay, communicate your thoughts gently. If all your judgment does is make someone feel bad, keep it to yourself.

Day 7: If you've been perpetuating a lie with yourself or someone else, today would be a good day to stop it. Come clean. Tell the truth.

Unique

Unique is a single bright, yellow dandelion in a field of lush green grass. It is the purple house standing proudly in a row of sedate white and gray homes. Unique is its own person. Unique doesn't look around to see what other people are doing. It doesn't care about fitting in. Unique is confident and content to be separate. In fact, it insists on being a one and only.

FOR THE FIRST THIRTY-SOME YEARS OF MY LIFE, I WORKED very hard to fit in. When I was in high school, for example, I tried not to do anything that would make me stand out. I made sure I had the "in" clothes. I made sure I talked about the right things and listened to the right music. The only thing I did that was remotely not "in" was get straight As, which was definitely not cool. Thank goodness I did that anyway.

Years later, in law school, it concerned me when I didn't study as much as my fellow classmates did. I didn't seem to need to spend as much time on the reading, and instead of enjoying this fact, I let it bother me. Because I was different, I figured I had to be doing something wrong.

This notion that I was wrong because I did tasks especially fast followed me into my thirties. Because I did most everything so much quicker than people I knew, I figured I must not have been doing what I did well. It bothered me that I was different from everyone else in this respect.

How silly is that? Here I have this ability to work quickly, and I'm ashamed of it? A few years ago, I finally made a perspective shift about this aspect of myself, and I began embracing and enjoying the fact that I work quickly. It's part of what makes me unique. Not to mention that it gives me more free time than I'd otherwise have.

When you're unique, you understand that you are you and no one else. When you're unique, you not only accept that you're different from others, you embrace the differences. You may join groups for companionship or some other purpose, but you don't need to be in a group to fit in.

Trying to fit in is draining. When you tamp down aspects of yourself so you won't call attention to yourself, you are taking energy that you could use to create your best life and instead using it to make yourself less than what you truly are. What you truly are is unique.

Everyone is unique. I don't care whether you look like a classic middle-aged mom or you drive the most popular car in the United States or you have the most common job. It doesn't matter whether you watch the popular TV shows and buy the best-selling foods in the grocery store. The combination of tastes, activities, and skills you have is what makes you unique.

Unlike its cousin qualities, free and independent, unique is a quality you don't actually have to cultivate. You're born with it. All you have to do is avoid squelching it. When you try to keep up with the styles, when you overemphasize being a "normal" member of society, you tend to distort the natural uniqueness with which you were born.

It's kind of like taking a beautifully, if exotically, decorated gingerbread boy and scraping off all the hot-pink-and-purple icing, the pistachio buttons, and the red-licorice hair. Once you take off the goodies, you're left with a plain old gingerbread boy. Ordinary. A cookie cutout. No longer unique.

This is what you do when you ignore your uniqueness. You get so caught up with having the right job, the right number of kids, and the right kind of body and hair, you forget about being the right kind of you.

Being unique means listening to rap music because you like it, even when all your friends are country music fans and they think rap music is stupid. When you're unique, you wear what you want, drive what you want, eat what you want, and not care a whit about looking stupid for doing something no one else does.

When you were born, you were iced with flair. If you want a quality life, you need to live in a way that shows off that icing. Be proud of it. Own it. Embrace it. Being unique is embracing the you of you. It's being who you are without a care about what other people think about it. Whatever you love to do, do it. Whatever you want to wear, wear it.

Celebrate the uniqueness of you.

౿ BECOMING UNIQUE

Day 1: Ask to be unique.

Day 2: Affirm your desire to become unique.

Day 3: Act as if you're unique.

Day 4: Tell yourself over and over, "I am a one and only." Smile every time you say it. Being a one and only is something to get excited about.

Day 5: If there's something about you that sets you apart from others, something you resist or don't like because you don't like being different (maybe you have a jerky walking gait or a high-pitched voice or a birthmark on your nose), instead of being ashamed of it and trying to hide it, embrace it. Thank whatever it is for making you unique.

Day 6: You probably have something in your life that others don't like but you love. For instance, maybe you have an odd piece of clothing that others think is tacky or maybe there's a song you love that others can't stand or maybe there's a food you love that others hate. Whatever the something is, wear it, listen to it, or eat it today.

Day 7: Make a list of all the things that set you apart from others. Include "good" and "bad" things. Read over the list. Feel good about the "good" things and make friends with the "bad" things. Be happy that everything about you makes you uniquely you. Take yourself out to dinner, alone. Celebrate your uniqueness.

Wise

Wise is the old man on the top of the mountain who has seen everything there is to see in life but is content to attach no judgment to anything he has seen. Wise knows no boundaries. It thinks in expanses of information and ideas. Wise knows how to think, and it knows how not to think when not thinking is the best thing to do. Wise is the serene glow that comes from knowing without needing to force knowledge on others.

MY HUSBAND, TIM, AND I PLAY A LOT OF SCRABBLE. WHEN we play, we use the dictionary quite a bit. Under the rules we've developed, it's okay to flip through it looking for words you can use. Some Scrabble aficionados would view this as cheating—but we see it as a way to make the game more fun as well as to expand our vocabulary because we learn new words every time we play.

One day, on one of my turns, I had the letters *Q, A, T, N, O, I,* and a blank. (The blank, for those of you who don't play Scrabble, can be any letter you want it to be.) When I drew the blank, I was thrilled. I'd had the *Q* for several turns and no *U* to go with it. The blank essentially gave me the *U* that I wanted.

Even though I now had the *Q* and *U* combination, I couldn't come up with a word that gave me any decent score. I kept thumbing through the *Q*s in the dictionary, and I couldn't find a word I could use. I was getting quite frustrated.

Still, I wasn't going to give up. I took a breath, sat back, and stared at my letters. That's when it hit me.

What if I didn't use the blank as a *U*? What if I made it something else?

I went back to the dictionary, and I found the word *qintar*. *Qintar* would fit on a spot on the board where I would get the *Q* tripled. If I used my blank as an *R*, not as a *U*, I could get a great score. So that's what I did.

Now, *Q* words almost always have a *U* in them. So conventional thinking would suggest my original reasoning, making the blank a *U*, would have given me the best result. It turned out this wasn't the case. In order to get the best result, I had to abandon conventional thinking and go with more expanded thinking, thinking that originated with a gut feeling from within. In other words, I had to *stop* thinking and *start* being wise.

Being wise isn't about racking up degrees so you can have a bunch of letters like B.A., Ph.D., or J.D. at the end of your name. It isn't about filling yourself up with facts, rules, and information. Being wise is about having a relaxed sense of knowing.

Being wise is, as advertisers like to call it, "thinking outside the box." It's a broad way of looking at the world, one that comes from the peace of awareness and acceptance. It is knowing from experience what does and doesn't work and being able to discern true choices when you face a situation that challenges you beyond what you already know.

Now, don't get me wrong. Knowledge is a fine thing. So are the letters you put after your name—I have a few of those myself, and I worked hard to earn them. These letters have helped me get jobs, and I'll admit I'm rather proud of them. However, they don't make me wise. All the books I've read, classes I've taken, and tapes I've listened to don't make me wise either.

So what does? I am wise more because of what I am than because of what I do.

Webster's Ninth New Collegiate Dictionary defines *wise* as, among other things, "marked by deep understanding, keen discernment, and a capacity for sound judgment." Where do understanding, discernment, and sound judgment come from? Can you get a degree in them? No. They come from within, either from intuitive knowing or from learning by experience.

When you develop yourself as a person who is aware of yourself and the world around you, when you pay attention to the natural order of the world and respect it, you will be wise. Wisdom is open. It's willing to discern what it doesn't see at first.

So how do you become wise if you're not?

Look around you; look with a flexible perception. Know that what you see now may not be all that is. Instead of pushing against the world, relax into it and let it show you what you need to know. The world, when viewed in this receptive way, will make you wise.

∽ Becoming Wise

Day 1: Ask to be wise.

Day 2: Affirm your desire to become wise.

Day 3: Act as if you're wise.

Day 4: Look around you. Pick something and stare at it for several minutes. Notice that when you first look at it, you'll see it in a different way than you will when you've looked at it for several minutes. Remind yourself that this shift in perception is available to you in every situation. It's what can help make you wise.

Day 5: Think of a problem you have. List at least three ways you could reframe the problem to see it differently. Is there perhaps a lesson in the problem? Look for it.

Day 6: Let go of any need to be right. Instead, be open to being wrong and finding wisdom in the mistake.

Day 7: If you're stuck in a project or in a life situation and you're thinking about it all the time, resolve not to think about it at all today. Giving your mind a rest can create new energy in your mind. This new energy creates the wisdom you need to move forward.

Joyful

Joyful is a burst of laughter, an exultant leap high into the air, and a whirl of delight. Joyful is a party, a celebration of life. Joyful is happiness squared. It is a big pot of tickled pink served up in a bowl made of sweet contentment. Joyful is a smile in the midst of pain and a hug in the midst of loneliness. Joyful is the candy of life.

SEVERAL YEARS AGO, MY FRIEND JAN SENT ME A BIRTHDAY card that so delighted me that I framed it. It hangs near the head of my bed where I can see it first thing in the morning when I wake up. Usually, I forget to look at it, having become so accustomed to it being there. But from time to time the picture catches my eye, and I linger over it.

The card's front is a print of a painting that depicts a little blonde girl with plump rosy cheeks. She's dressed in a pink-flowered pinafore over a polka-dot white blouse, and she's running across a grassy field. Her hair blows around her head. Her arms are thrown wide, and she clutches a colorful bouquet of wildflowers in her right hand. At her left side, running alongside her, is a small white and brown terrier-type dog with a little stick in its mouth. The dog's tail is up and wagging, and its eyes are bright. The girl's face is lit up by the sunshine glowing around her and her dog, and her joy is evident in her wide, sweet smile.

The card itself is a birthday card with a simple wish to have a fun day. Jan wrote, "dear precious Andrea" under the "Happy Birthday." For some reason, the card in combination with the words *dear* and *precious* made me think of the joy within me. It reminded me that when I allow myself to do so, I can exult in life just like the little girl on the front of the card is doing. I think the girl on this card embodies what it means to be joyful.

Being joyful is delighting in life. It's rejoicing in our experiences. It's pure happiness—bliss. It's what we are meant to be, yet most of us aren't.

Life as an adult can be challenging. Most of us need to earn a living. We need to take care of ourselves and maybe children, aging parents, or a spouse. We need to keep our house clean and our refrigerator stocked. We need to cook, run errands, pay bills, and do taxes. This is not the stuff of a joyful outlook on life. This is often drudgery. Or at least, that's how most people treat it.

But being joyful doesn't require sunshine, a grassy field, a bouquet of wildflowers, a frilly dress, and a cute little dog with a wagging tail. It doesn't need perfect, beautiful surroundings or even perfect, delightful experiences. Being joyful is not about what is going on around you. It's about what's going on inside you.

Of course, you can wait to be joyful. You can wait for everything in your life to go perfectly. You can wait for those extraordinary days—your wedding, a perfect Christmas, a special birthday, the birth of your child, the success of your business, the building of your dream house. You can wait to have great health and good fortune. You can wait until you have all you desire. You can put off feeling joyful until all your personal ducks are lined up in a happy little row.

But I have troublesome news for you. If you wait, you may never get to experience feeling joyful. And if you never feel joyful, you have less chance of lining up all your personal ducks. A life without joy rarely bursts forth with extraordinary days, great health, good fortune, and all you desire. A life without joy tends to bring more of the same: no joy.

Most of us tend to go around looking for joy in our lives. This is an ironic and pointless search because joy isn't out there someplace. It's in here, inside of us. Joy is our natural essence. Just as a Tootsie Pop doesn't look for chewy chocolate because it already has chewy chocolate at its core, we have no need to look for joy. Joy is our chewy chocolate center. It is naturally revealed when we allow it.

Being joyful, then, is not about seeking joy but about removing barriers to joy. We become blocked from joy when we get stuck in fear, anger, envy, frustration, and all the other ego-driven emotions that drain life from our lives. Developing and using the qualities in this book removes these barriers to joy. When you remove the barriers, you open a window within yourself that allows you to find that joyful core. It's a window that looks out to a grassy field kissed by sunshine and dotted with beautiful wildflowers.

To drop the heavy barriers that separate you from the joy that already lies within you, start with pleasure. Look for it in all you do. Then savor it. Now add a sense of gratitude to your day. Appreciate your life. Sprinkle in a feeling of being happy you're alive. Mix in all the inner qualities you've developed. Stir it all with a smile. This is your recipe for being joyful.

Here's an example of how this works: I'm feeling discouraged because something I expected didn't happen. The discouragement is like a heavy weight pressing down on me. It's a barrier to joy. Realizing that I've disconnected from my joyful self, I look around and see my husband, Tim, singing as he washes dishes in our kitchen. I *focus* on the crinkles around his eyes that I so love. I am *grateful* for his willingness to help around the house. Using just these two qualities, I bring myself back to the pleasure of the moment, and the barrier put up by discouragement falls. Now I'm feeling appreciation for having such a wonderful husband, and I feel happy about the great life I lead. I smile. And there it is—the window to joy opens within, and I feel delight, happiness, and bliss.

Every day presents dozens of opportunities to cuddle up to delight, happiness, and bliss. When you're joyful, you don't miss any of those chances. You jump through the window that looks out to your field of joy and you seize them all, clutching them like a bouquet of wildflowers as you run with abandon through the grassy field of your life.

ꙮ Becoming Joyful

Day 1: Ask to be joyful.

Day 2: Affirm your desire to become joyful.

Day 3: Act as if you're joyful.

Day 4: Find pleasure in all you do today. Use whatever quality you need to use to look for even the smallest pleasures. Now savor them.

Day 5: Be conscious of all the wonderful things you have in your life. Say often "_____ brings me joy." Fill in the blank with as many different things as possible throughout the day.

Day 6: Be happy. No matter what's going on, be happy you're breathing.

Day 7: Every time you go to the bathroom today, imagine being a child running with happy abandon through a field of wildflowers. This will make you smile. Let that smile lead you to being joyful.

Notes

1. Esmond Wright, *Franklin of Philadelphia* (Cambridge, Mass.: Harvard University Press, 1986), 46.

2. *A Course in Miracles* (Tiburon, Calif.: Foundation for Inner Peace, 1975).

3. Isabel Allende, "The Creators—How They Keep Going and Going and . . . ," interview by Joseph Dumas, *AARP Modern Maturity* (March/April 2002), 39.

4. Robert Karen, "The Power of Apology," *O, The Oprah Magazine* (February 2001): 71–74, 188.

5. Lisa Curdy, "Cash Blows into Traffic in Central Park," *The Daily World*, 24 August 2002, A7.

6. Christiane Northrup, *Health Wisdom for Women*, vol. 9, no. 8 (August 2002).

7. Lynn A. Robinson, *Divine Intuition: Your Guide to Creating a Life You Love* (New York: Dorling Kindersley Publishing Inc., 2001), 17.

8. Susan Donahue, "Hard Work, Optimism Help Him Cope with Rare Affliction," *The Daily World*, 9 October 2000, A8.

9. David Gardner and Tom Gardner, *The Motley Fool Investment Guide* (New York: Fireside, 2001).

10. Jean-Dominique Bauby, *The Diving Bell and the Butterfly* (New York: Vintage, 1997).

About the Author

Andrea Rains Waggener is a writer of fiction and nonfiction. Her newspaper column, "The Up Beat," has inspired people for more than five years to live an upbeat, quality life. She lives with her husband and dog near the coast in the state of Washington. You can visit Andrea on the Web at www.waggener-books.com.